AWARENESS IS ARMOR

Learn to Defend Yourself Online and in Real Time

ALEXANDRA ALLRED

Wish
PUBLISHING

Wish Publishing
Terre Haute, Indiana
www.wishpublishing.com

Proofread by Kathy Pickrell
Cover designed by Phil Velikan

Printed in the United States of America
10 9 8 7 6 5 4 3 2 1

Published in the United States by
Wish Publishing
P.O. Box 10337
Terre Haute, IN 47801, USA
www.wishpublishing.com

For those in need of greater self-esteem, emotional and/or physical security. You are worth fighting for! This book – *Awareness is Armor* – says it all. You are worth the fight. You are not alone. You are never alone.

Never be afraid to speak up; never be afraid to fight.

Table of Contents

PREFACE
What are We Fighting For?

You are stronger than you think. The key to defending yourself is to believe in yourself. It is that simple. As you read real-life scenarios in the following pages, you will meet victims of sexual harassment and/or assault who reacted to these aggressions in very different ways. Those who spoke up were often verbally attacked by others in their defense of the assailant, while victims who remained quiet then suffered in silence.

We must take better care of ourselves. We must love and respect ourselves better than we have. More importantly, we must start supporting one another.

Knowing how to defend yourself does not mean picking fights or becoming a bully. Quite the opposite. Learning how to defend yourself translates to greater self-esteem and self-worth which then lends to greater compassion and empathy toward others.

Why look for trouble?

Why pick fights just to be argumentative?

If you can walk away, then walk away. This is basic self-defense 101.

On April 26, 2016, Trinity Carr, 16, and two of her friends decided to attack Amy Joyner-Francis in their school bathroom while others watched and recorded the fight on their phones. It was no fight. Blindsided by the first punch, Amy went down and never had a chance. She died, gasping for breath, in the handicap stall of the bathroom. Between the combination of the assault and a rare heart condition no one knew about, Amy's life ended when she was just 16 years old on the floor of a school bathroom for reasons she probably never understood. [1]

---

1. *https://www.usatoday.com/story/news/nation-now/2017/04/13/verdict-delaware-teen-fatal-school-bathroom-fight/100415104/*

Kaitlin Leonor Castilleja, 18, on the other hand, died in the backseat of a car while she bled out from a knife wound to the neck following a social media feud with a 16-year-old girl.[2]

For what?

While this information is really heavy (and depressing), it is real life. These girls were once vibrant and very much alive but now they are gone.

Fights, whether physical or cyber, are almost always pointless. A fight over a boy, a car, a comment made online or over a phone does not make you who and what you are, but one stupid fight – one stupid fight that goes wrong – can ruin and even take your life. So, let's talk about kinds of fights that **do** matter:

- Fighting Bullying
- Fighting Cyber Attacks and CyberBullying
- Fighting an Assailant (both physically or in the legal system)

Right away, we will tackle these important topics, but there are other worthy fights to take up in defense of yourself:

- Fighting Personal Negativity
- Fighting Peer Pressure
- Fighting Image Saboteurs
- Fighting Media Images
- Fighting Social Injustices

HOW THIS BOOK WAS DESIGNED FOR YOU TO READ

As humans are visual creatures, most of us (approximately 65%) are visual learners, but in the sports, fitness, martial arts and self-defense world, understanding the why of a particular movement is critical to a physical skill set or execution. Therefore this book outlines real case scenarios in which you are asked to consider what just happened, what the victim might have done to escape harm, and how you might have reacted in that same scenario.

---

2. *https://www.expressnews.com/news/education/article/Witnesses-to-fatal-night-in-San-Antonio-are-still-13726682.php#photo-17146823*

It is recommended that you read this book with others and have an open discussion to answer those very questions. It is also very important to note that while the vast majority of scenarios in this book involve females as the victim or potential victim, boys and men are also the victims of sexual harassment and assault.

A study in April (Sexual Assault Awareness Month) of 2020 revealed that 1 in every 6 boys is sexually assaulted by his 18th birthday.[3] Even in 2020, the stigma attached to a male victim can be debilitating. As you will read in Chapter 16: Male Survivors of Sexual Assault, even a big strong, powerful man such as actor Terry Crews can be subjected to online bullying when he revealed his own #MeToo experience. Given the magnitude of these assaults and importance of empowering everyone, it is our hope to produce a sequel to this book, in which the 'What Would You Do?' scenarios are directed specifically to male readers.

As the title of this book suggests, you are learning to defend yourself. *Awareness is Armor* is about protecting yourself in all ways, from physical and emotional abuse to negative pressure you may feel from peers in person and on social media, from media images, even from family and your own feelings of self-worth.

Let's go!

---

3. *Dube SR, Anda RF, Whitfield CL, et al. Long-term consequences of childhood sexual abuses by gender of victim. Am J Prev Med. 2005: 430-438.*

1

WHAT DOES YOUR "BAD GUY" LOOK LIKE?

What does your "bad guy" look like? We all have an idea in our minds of what a bad guy or scary person looks like. However silly or unrealistic it may seem, we have preconceived ideas. Is he tall? Muscular? Menacing looking? Maybe he's shorter with a thicker-build and creepy smile.

Is he a he?

Maybe your bad guy isn't even a man. While the majority of scenarios in this book highlight female victims, please note that males are also victim of sexual assault, harassment, and bullying. Chapter 16 specifically details statistical information about male victims but each of the scenarios in this book can and should be applied to males as well.

For most people, however, there is an image conjured from a scary movie or a picture from the news of a man, covered in tattoos and snarling into the camera.

Whatever he or she looks like, take the image in your mind and toss it out the window. As you read in the Preface, two different 16-year-old girls were responsible for the deaths of their victims. Be honest. When you hear that a 16- or 18-year-old girl is killed, you probably never consider the *bad guy* was another girl.

Across the nation, a rash of school shootings have revealed that classmates, from ages as young as 12, have opened fire on their peers, most of whom never harmed, teased or bullied the shooter in any way. On Valentine's Day 2019, a former classmate returned to his school in Parkland, FL, to kill 17 students, injuring dozens, simply because he was angry. It is hard to fathom that one of our new *bad guys* can be categorized as a high school boy or girl, but it is true.

Crimes committed by women, according to the FBI, are also on the rise. Women are engaging in more theft and violent crimes than ever before. We, as a people, are changing, and not for the better.

The hard truth is a 'bad guy' can be very young or old, male or female, tall or short, black or white or of Asian, Latin, Middle Eastern or Caribbean descent. This 'bad guy' can be a neighbor, relative, teacher or total stranger. Because there are so many varied descriptions of the 'bad guy,' it is all the more important to focus on the victim. As we identify the characteristics of a victim, it allows us to assess our own strengths and weaknesses in the hope of not becoming one, and, if we once were, learning how to come back stronger than ever before.

WHAT IS A VICTIM?

A victim is anyone who has suffered injury or loss of property from an accident, a natural disaster, a crime or disease. A victim is a person or animal adversely affected by an action or circumstance. A victim is someone who has been tricked, duped, conned or exploited for the personal gains of another.

In self-defense, however, the term becomes a little more defined. A victim is someone who has been assaulted either by a stranger or by a known associate. This can and does make things very confusing for the victim when the assailant is known to the victim. The consequences of assault are complicated, with long-reaching effects on mental and physical health, personal relationships, professional careers, school, or even sports and religion. Victims are often left with the question, "Why," to which there is rarely an answer.

Sound confusing? Oh, it is. And the attacker, the 'bad guy,' plans on using that confusion to his or her advantage.

STOP THE SELF-SABOTAGE

We hear the "love yourself" mantra so often that it is easy to dismiss its importance, but the truth is, it is a great self-defense tool.

- An ideal victim for a predator is one who is full of self-doubt and a poor self-image.
- Predators seek out potential victims who are too nice to say no and feel the need to please.

In particular, predators who live amongst us, coach, teach or work with their potential victims require two qualities: trust and insecurities. With this formula, the predator can lavish praise on a person who might not otherwise feel deserving of such attention while also, very subtly, tearing their victim down. This teacher, coach, neighbor, relative, pastor, coworker or supposed friend will tell their victim how wonderful, beautiful or amazing they are while also reminding them that "you're lucky to have me" and "other people don't understand you the way I do." It's called "grooming."

GROOMING

Your bad guy may be someone you don't even recognize as a bad guy because you know him or her so well! That is, you *thought* you knew this person so well. Your trust blinds you to the fact that you are being groomed.

Grooming is a slow, methodical process in which an offender (a bad guy you do not yet understand is a bad guy) pulls his or her victim into a sexual but secret relationship. The process can be so slow that a person does not understand what is happening. In the multiple cases of R&B singer R. Kelly, teenage girls and young women truly thought they were in consenting relationships with the singer. Later, they admitted that they were verbally, physically, and sexually abused by R. Kelly. They were manipulated and lied to but, at the time, thought it was part of their 'relationship.' Oprah Winfrey has long shared stories of being manipulated and abused by a family member while actor Finn Wolfhard, from "Stranger Things," shared that he was abused by his agent at the age of 14.

In 2018, fans of the Christian-based country band, The Willis Clan, were stunned to learn that the father, the patriarch of the group, had been raping his own daughters, carefully grooming each girl, for decades. When the band, consisting of 12 children, first gained international fame on "America's Got Talent," several of the daughters were already Toby Willis' victims. Not until daughter Jessica Willis began to speak out did her sisters also reveal they, too, had been raped by their own father for decades.[1]

---

1. *https://www.christianpost.com/news/toby-willis-daughter-jessica-reveals-decades-sex-abuse-beatings-secrets-christian-family.html*

Why did the daughters not first speak up when they had the world's attention in 2014? Why didn't the sisters talk to each other before that? Where was the mother?

As you will read, groomers know how to attack and manipulate, and they rely on silence and shame.

Groomers, i.e. predators, can be anyone from a teacher, a doctor, an agent, a relative, a friend's parent or a priest, even a follower on Instagram. A groomer can be anyone who establishes him or herself in a position of trust, then friendship. In defense of yourself, here's what you need to know about predatory grooming:

1. GROOMING YOU

Victims can be young children or older adults. What the groomer relies upon is the victim's silence. In one particular story, a grandfather of three girls molested two of the three. He was able to manipulate the two girls so that each one stayed silent in her own confusion and shame. After nearly two decades of his abuse when the truth was revealed, their grandmother, who had suspected something was happening but had also been groomed to remain silent, revealed that the only reason the third sister had never been a victim was because the grandfather knew she would never remain silent. Groomers *select* their prey.

2. GROOMING TRUST

When we hear the words 'victim' and 'assault,' we think instant and aggressive. The reality is groomers take their time, laying the groundwork of friendship and trust which can take place online, in a classroom, on an athletic field, or in the home. Over a course of time, the groomer learns about your personal life, your insecurities, fears, and passions, and then uses that information to manipulate you and your emotions.

3. GROOMING FAVORS

Whether the groomer is a coach offering more play time, a teacher offering better grades, or a neighbor promising a car or cash or any kind of promise that makes you feel special, these favors are a way for the predator to ingratiate him or herself to you. The idea, always, is to make you feel grateful so that the friendship can escalate to a sexual relationship. More sophisticated groomers will move slowly, even making their victim feel like the progression of a relationship is your idea.

4. GROOMING SECRETS

"Let's not tell anyone about this," and "Other people won't understand" are code for "We should keep this a secret." While many young people find this kind of secrecy intimate and/or exciting, it is all part of the groomer's tactic to isolate his or her victim from friends, family, counselors, etc.

5. GROOMING ROMANCE

Secrecy in place, the groomer becomes a very clever *sexual partner*. The victim, concealing this relationship from the outside world, is far more likely to think and believe that this new romance is real, special, exclusive. It is how teachers or adult neighbors convince their victim to 'run away' with them because "no one will understand." True love, as with any real friendship, should include all your loved ones and friends, not exclude them.

6. GROOMERS LOSE WHEN VICTIMS SPEAK UP

If telling the truth can mean the end of that "relationship," it's time to talk. It is important to know that talking means ... to anyone. If you do not feel that you can tell a friend or family member or are too embarrassed to share, call the **National Domestic Violence Hotline** (800-799-7233) or the **Victim Connect Resource Center** (855-4-VICTIM or 855-484-2846) to speak to a professional who cannot and will not judge you.

7. GROOMERS VS. FAMILY & FRIENDS

As groomers focus on secrecy, family and friends may see a change. For younger victims, sudden bedwetting can be a sign while nightmares, sudden changes in behaviors, including risk-taking, diet, exercise, anxiety, depression, even suicidal thoughts and/or withdrawal from normal activities and friends can all be signs of victimization. Friends and family can be crucial in saving someone from abuse by speaking up. In fact, the very hotlines previously listed can also help advise friends and family who suspect something might be going on.[2]

There is no specific *look* a predator (or groomer) has but their behaviors, operating in secrecy while offering favors and gifts, are identifiable. Learning to identify behaviors may be one of the most

---

2. *https://www.allure.com/story/what-is-sexual-grooming-abuse*

important aspects of self-protection and self-defense, followed by speaking out.

As you will later read, learning to use your own voice is empowering and can save your life.

2

THE BEHAVIORS
OF A BAD GUY

This cannot be said enough times: Aggressive, unwanted behaviors are not about you. These behaviors are for and about the predator. He or she does not care about you. Predators are opportunists. That is, if they believe they can get away with manipulating and/or harming you, they do so because it is part of their own game. You, your appearance, your charm, etc., mean nothing to them.

Who is the Aggressor/Predator and What are the Signs to Look For?

There are no hard-and-fast rules when it comes to what a sexual predator looks like, but there are some general behaviors and attitudes that are typical with most. They are:

- Aggressors tend to be immature.

- Aggressors tend to be bullies, often in a passive/aggressive manner.

- Aggressors tend to be bad losers. They cannot accept 'no,' rejection or disapproval.

- Aggressors tend to become overly emotional about issues and are easily frustrated.

- Aggressors miss common social cues about personal space or proper etiquette.

- Aggressors rarely take responsibility for their own actions and often blame others.

- In the event of "evidence," aggressors tend to claim the evidence or truths are false, made up, or conjured.

- Aggressors display a lack of empathy or understanding in regards to other people's feelings.

- Aggressors are self-centered.

- Aggressors are often entitled or possess a sense of entitlement.

- Aggressors crave power and always have to be in control. They may often yell over others to be heard and, even as adults, throw tantrums.

- Not surprisingly, aggressors often display sexually deviant behaviors and/or attitudes, such as blurting out a person's physical attributes or how a woman should be handled in front of other people, including other women.

- And aggressors justify mean-spirited comments; they justify sexually explicit remarks about women; they justify demeaning comments about women: *She had that coming… but you would never be like that.*

Of course, they will deny any responsibility for hurting another person. In the beginning, they may often say things, "I was only kidding," and "It was just a joke. You need to stop taking everything so seriously." They will convince their victim (and others) that they were simply misunderstood. "I didn't mean it that way." As part of their "it's not my fault!" disguise, aggressors are masters of deflection. There is a reason why people always say, "I had no idea! He seemed like such a nice guy!" when learning a neighbor, friend, or teacher is a sexual predator. Aggressors are often:

- Married, a family-man, or "a really nice guy"

- Entrenched in their community as a trusted member

- Given to "jokes" about girls or women and/or objectifying women but always appearing light-hearted and harmless

- Able to gain trust through familiarity

- There to offer a shoulder to lean on in times of crisis as this allows them to insinuate themselves in the community, the family, the workplace and, ultimately, into your personal life. They are often – belatedly – described as someone you could count on.

The deceptive, deflective nature of predators leads to one of the more dangerous and ridiculous myths: "He's very wealthy and successful. Why would he need to attack someone? He could get any woman he wants!" A predator's wealth, status, or charm has nothing to do with a predatory nature. Serial rapist and murderer Ted Bundy was successful in luring his victims *because* he was charming, educated, and socially-connected. For the predator, assaulting victims is a game and has nothing to do with money, status, education or, for that matter, you.

And now you're thinking, "Well, that's just great. Who can I trust?"

You need to learn to trust *you*! In the coming chapters, we will discuss why girls and women do not listen enough to their own instincts and how to change that. But, before we do that, we must dispel the myths of why girls and women *deserve* to be victims.

3

THE BEHAVIORS
OF A VICTIM

Why don't more victims report a crime of assault when it happens? Statistically speaking, if the victim knows the attacker, a crime is reported just 18 to 30% of the time. If the attacker is a stranger, victims report the assault just half of the time. Why?

Sadly, there is a long history as to why victims are fearful about speaking up about sexual assault. Because sexual crimes are about power, not sex, most victims remain fearful even when the attack, the crime, is over. They do not believe the police can protect them; they do not believe their attacker can or will be punished.

WARNING: The following story is hard to read but it brings home the point of how irresponsible, outdated beliefs about victims cause more harm than help.

In 2014, a Montana judge made the news when he blamed a 14-year old victim for her own rape. Judge G. Todd Baugh sentenced a school teacher who raped his student to only 30 days in jail because the girl, the victim, "seemed older than her chronological age" and was "as much in control of the situation" as her attacker. As a result, the 14-year old girl later committed suicide.[1] And while the judge was later suspended, the damage was done, also reinforcing to many more victims that reporting a crime was not worth the humiliation and retaliation.

Victims fear hearing:

- If she was really raped, why did it take her so long to tell anyone?

- Women cry rape when they regret having sex or are embarrassed.

- She's just looking for attention!

---

1. *https://www.theatlantic.com/politics/archive/2014/06/the-montana-judge-who-blamed-a-14-year-old-for-her-own-rape-will-be-censured/372185/*

- She knew what she was getting in to …
- What woman goes to a guy's room to 'talk'?
- Did you see how she was dressed?
- If she was really raped, she would have called the police.

In reality, only 2% of all rape and related sex charges are false (or falsified), whereas only about 40% of all rapes are ever reported to the authorities.

The good news is attitudes about assault and victims are improving with education but more changes need to occur. Below are some of the main reasons victims still do not speak up for themselves:

Why Victims Avoid Reporting

- Victims know their report will become public and they are already devastated and humiliated.
- Victims fear further shame/embarrassment from public scrutiny regarding their personal lives, from how they dress, where they work, who they were with, etc.
- Victims fear how family will react.
- Victims fear their aggressor (and fear retribution from a boss, neighbor, friend, or family member).
- Victims are further confused/ashamed when the aggressor is someone they know and loved/liked/trusted.

In particular, when the attacker is in a position of power like a teacher, coach, boss, even an athlete or celebrity, the fear is that there will not be a conviction in favor of the victim. Today, however, with more police and support groups, women's organizations and educators standing up, so, too, are victims.

Your Role in the It's-the-Victim's-Fault Mentality

Have you ever said, "She had it coming," to a friend or even thought it? Why?

In the last year or even in the last week, how many times have you heard a radio, television, or online personality roast a woman for what she wore, how she looked or acted? Does that same personality say the same sorts of things about how men look or act? No, right?

YOUR ROLE IN ACTION AND RECOVERY

Because victims may feel responsible for what happened to them, berating themselves for their lack of judgment or not seeing the signs, they do not report the attack. They may believe because they drank too much or because of what they wore or how they behaved, they somehow deserved to be assaulted. Additionally, they may fear what their parents, friends or co-workers will think of them.

Not only is this wrong, but how can they possibly heal from the long-term emotional wounds if they keep the assault a secret?

This is where friends and family do have a say in recovery and reporting. When you tell a victim, "I believe you," it just may be the most powerful healing tool you can offer. This tells your friend or your loved one that they must not feel ashamed or afraid. By saying, "It's not your fault," "You did not deserve this," and "You are not alone," you give them the courage to help themselves and others.

The road to recovery for survivors of assault can be long and difficult but, with a strong support base of friends and family and bringing in supportive professionals and police, the victim can become empowered once more. By sharing their trauma, they can heal.

It is okay to say, "I'm sorry this happened to you," to acknowledge what happened, and to promise "I'm here for you." The more the victim speaks, the stronger she or he will become.

4

HOW DID I NOT SEE THAT COMING?
The Cyber Bad Guy

As we talk about self-esteem, self-worth, and self-defense, we must discuss self-awareness. You cannot truly care about yourself if you do not have self-awareness.

AWARENESS

The #1 asset a person can have to help prevent an assault is awareness. You have heard this statement a hundred times: *Be aware of your surroundings!* But how many times have you walked into a parking lot talking on the phone or sat in your car fiddling with makeup? How often have you been so lost in deep thought in public that you were unaware of your surroundings? How often have you gone for a walk or gone jogging with your music turned up just a little too loudly? How often have you struggled to carry groceries from your car to the front door, barely aware of who is there, in your quest to limit your trips between the car and house?

We've all done it.

We tell ourselves that being aware of our surroundings is only necessary when in an unfamiliar place or when you get a creepy vibe from someone. Right?

Wrong. Situational awareness and self-awareness are a constant, never-ending aspect of survival and self-defense. In fact, most women are assaulted in a known, comfortable environment such as their home, on campus, in the home of a friend, or the office, i.e., a place where their guard is down.

WHAT IS SELF-AWARENESS?

It is not enough to just be situationally aware; you must also be self-aware. Self-awareness is recognizing yourself as an individual in your environment (whatever and wherever that is) in the physical sense but also identifying your own traits, or your personality, to include your strengths and weaknesses, fears and beliefs, and how you respond to different situations. Self-awareness does not just include yourself but how you interact with other people and how they perceive and receive you. In self-defense, this self-awareness is how a predator may come to choose you as a victim. Though most aggressors are opportunists, they are (cowards, by nature) more apt to choose a victim who will not fight. How you present yourself (i.e., how you see yourself) and how the world sees you (i.e., how you present yourself) are critical in survival and self-defense.

AWARENESS ON SOCIAL MEDIA

In the beginning of the book, two kinds of *bad guys* were identified: Those you know and those who are complete strangers. However, the Internet has created a new kind of bad guy – meet the cyber bad guy or, as you may think of him/her, your cyber friend.

Your cyber friend is safe because of the buffer. He or she is someone with whom you've become familiar with inside jokes, shared emojis, and seemingly innocent bits of personal information. But for a predator, every little thing you post, every image, every smile, every shared 'like' is gathered up to be used against you. Let's take a better look at the cyber predator.

BEWARE: THE CYBER PREDATOR

Guess what? There's an excellent chance you've got an online 'friend' who is actually a cyber predator. More than 95% of all American teens between the ages of 12 to 17 are online with a Smartphone, and at least one in every five U.S. teenagers report they have received unwanted sexual solicitation via social media. Let's face it: With those odds, someone with predatory tendencies may very well be looking at your personal profile.

Internet sexual predators, ages 18 to 55, most often target teens between the ages of 11 and 15. In **100** of the cases, teens who became victims of sexual online predators willingly met with them (a reminder of how powerful the grooming process can be), and **75%** of underage online users are willing to share personal information about themselves or their families if they believe they can win a prize or have access to an online game.[1]

While debates continue among pediatricians, psychologists, and politicians on whether video games cause more aggressive/violent behaviors, we do know that video games can create, or certainly exacerbate, depression, anxiety and lowered self-esteem, particularly among adolescents and younger teens, making the grooming process for online predators even easier in finding their next victim.[2]

And the favorite targets for the online predators? Bored girls. In 2015, a group of men from Michigan, Florida, Texas, Ohio, North Carolina, Pennsylvania, California, and Ontario, Canada, all formed an online chat room which ensnared a "bored" 14-year-old girl into performing sexual acts online. The girl believed she was performing for just one interested boy while, in fact, her very personal acts were being viewed by men all over the Internet.

"I'M Soooo BORED"

When the FBI finally brought down this particular online sexual exploitation ring, known as the "Bored Group," federal investigators discovered that the group had actually encrypted the words "bored," "just bored," "borednstff," "f*bored," "boredascanbe," and "soooobored" to find potential victims. Using dozens of chat-rooms, the predators moved in, also pretending to be bored teenagers.

"If a girl was suicidal or revealed that she was cutting herself, the group engaged in what they called a "trust building session." Trust building sessions involved no discussion of sexual activity, but rather more sensitive chats about life and the child's worth," the U.S. Attorney documents stated, because "the group used trust building as an opportunity to further engender loyalty to the group so as to increase the chances that the girl would later engage in sexual activity on web camera."[3] They groomed her.

---

1. https://www.puresight.com/Pedophiles/Online-Predators/online-predators-statistics.html

2. https://www.ncbi.nlm.nih.gov/pmc/articles/PMC6676913/

3. https://www.pressconnects.com/story/news/public-safety/2018/12/03/online-predators-internet-sexual-enticement-children-cyber-crime-protect/1820834002/

While the focus of this story is on girls, it is important to note that 30% of victims of Internet sexual exploitation are boys and those numbers are rising. The combination of restlessness or boredom with a false sense of cyber security (*If I'm in my own room, I am safe.*) is dangerous for males and females of all ages.

THERE ARE NO SECRETS ONLINE

Instagram, just one of several social media formats with over a billion users, is the perfect place for aspiring actors, singers and models who have opted for the "business" setting on their personal account to get their information, they hope, into the right hands. Unfortunately, with more than 500,000 sexual predators online everyday[4], what hands (and eyes) really access the information?

Even those who simply want to post silly, fun pictures of themselves playing sports, eating, or just hanging out with friends expose more about themselves than they intend. Predators pay attention. They see locations, names of schools or restaurants, and compile information about where a boy or girl lives or attends school. From there, making a connection by name-dropping someone the intended victim knows and/or bringing up common interests can open up dialogue. From there, the hunter begins his dangerous game.

Instead of making things more difficult for the criminal, however, and despite what we all know about sexual predators and cyber thieves, we continue to offer more personal information online than ever.

THE 'SOCIAL INFLUENCER' DANGERS

The "influencer," for example, in his/her quest to win over more followers and gain fame, also invites problems. In October 2019, a man in Japan was charged with assault after he used his victim's Instagram selfies to hunt her down. How? He used the reflection in her eyes from a selfie she had taken at her local train station to locate her.

A man in California hunted down a 12-year-old girl from the photos she posted of herself in a dance studio while many, many more use updated Instagram, Facebook, and Twitter posts to stalk victims while they are out having fun with friends or family.

---

4. *https://patch.com/massachusetts/sudbury/bp—stats-about-online-predators-and-precautions-parec47b01a336*

When influencer Andreea Cristina's cyber-stalker first began to send her messages through personal emails he had found, then sent a letter to her mother's home address, she refused to respond. She had never believed looking into a camera, safe in her own room, could bring trouble to her home, let alone her mother's doorstep. The more she ignored him, however, the angrier he became, finally outright threatening her. "He said, 'I found your address, and if you think that you're just going to keep ignoring me, I'm going to come and find you.' He actually came good on his threats," Cristina said. Ultimately, she had to hire a private investigator to find her stalker to have a restraining order issued.

There have always been cases of fans who stalk a TV or movie star, believing they were 'destined' to be together. Terrifying but true. Known as "parasocial interaction," created in the 1950s, the illusion of a relationship between a celebrity or even fictional character becomes very real to the viewer.[5] Today, however, those illusions have become stronger because, thanks to social media, celebrities can and do actually interact with fans. Here's how it works:

A YouTube vlogger, Instagram influencer, or high-profile Twitter user shares personal thoughts and feelings, allowing fans to respond. A simple 'follow back' or 'like' from the online celebrity brings illusion to life and the fan is certain that this is a friendship and/or relationship. When, however, the celebrity doesn't respond to the fan on a regular basis or the fan disapproves of something the celebrity has done or said, the fan feels betrayed. The online celebrity, of course, has no idea.

In September 2013, a woman was arrested after the Royal Canadian Mounted Police were able to track her IP addresses to a tiny town called Easterville in the province of Manitoba, after she nearly destroyed the careers and lives of NBA basketball player Chris "Birdman" Andersen and a rising online media star 17-year-old Paris Dunn. Simply for sport, a recluse named Shelly Chartier decided it would be fun to stalk Andersen and Dunn and create a relationship between the two. In doing so, Chartier endangered the life of Dunn, brought about public shame and scrutiny for both Dunn and Andersen, and nearly got Andersen imprisoned.

Because Chartier was lonely and friendless, she got into the *sport* of "catfishing" (when a person uses internet profiles to interact with other

---

5. *https://www.psychologytoday.com/us/blog/your-online-secrets/201607/youre-not-really-friends-internet-celebrity*

people online) to degrade and humiliate others for her own entertainment.[6]

Thanks to cyber thieves and sexual perverts, catfishers and online celebrity "fans," there is a huge and dangerous online population out there that makes it impossible for you to know and identify what the *bad guy* looks like. That is why you must be self-aware.

Self-defense and self-awareness, as you will learn, are about both who and what is out there in the real world and who and what might be lurking online. Because just as influencer Andreea Cristina's bad guy appeared in person, so, too, have many others. Today, cyber-stalking and in-person stalking are both on the rise globally. More than 25% of teens have reported that online incidents later resulted in some kind of face-to-face confrontation.[7]

A note about your cyber stalker: This lurking person who likes to post creepy or cruel things about you is, statistically speaking, probably someone you know. Over 75% of victims know their stalker, with approximately 30% of the stalkers being an ex-partner or friend.[8]

Before we go on, it is also necessary to talk about online gaming.

By 2015, more than 40% of gamers were female and the non-gaming world was becoming aware of how violent video gamers are toward their female opponents. The macho environment in the games and depictions of buxom females, all very anti-female, allowed for a culture in which very un-macho, stereotypical males who would typically be bullied by their own male peers in everyday life, made repeated threats against women. In the documentary *GTFO*, filmmaker Shannon Sun-Higginson reveals just how bad sexual harassment is against female gamers, and how extremely reluctant those female gamers are to complain for fear of losing their positions (or ranking as gamers) within the industry.[9] While a skilled male gamer may be called harmless names, most laden with comical yet respectful remarks, similarly skilled female

---

6. *https://abcnews.go.com/Technology/nba-star-aspiring-model-victims-massive-catfishing-scheme/story?id=46755887*

7. *https://www.pewresearch.org/internet/2011/11/09/teens-kindness-and-cruelty-on-social-network-sites/*

8. *https://nij.ojp.gov/topics/articles/voices-field-stalking*

9. *Crisell, Hattie, "What Female Gamers Want You to Know About Being Abused Online," BuzzFeed. February 17, 2016.*

gamers are met with something quite different and disturbing. The following remarks were directed to just one successful female gamer in just one example:

- "@____, I violently masturbated to your face on your latest video."
- "@____, I'll rape you and put your head on a stick"
- "@____, suck' ma dick, u a slut"
- "Why don't you kill yourself and make a video about it?"
- "The only place for women is in chains in my kitchen."
- "@____, suck my c#@# and cook me a steak."
- "Wouldn't it be funny if five guys raped her right now?"
- "Why did the feminist cross the road ... TO SUCK MY D#%#."[10]

Even in the cyber world, even among some of the most stereotypically geeky men on earth, women are belittled and degraded as entertainment. The idea is simple: Bully and threaten until women leave and, if they stay, they must like it.

There is that long-held belief that women secretly like aggressive behavior in the way of sexual assault. This is both ridiculous and dangerous. In the case of these predatory gamers (most hiding in their own basements), many instances of online abuse escalated to revealing female gamers cell phone numbers, home addresses and other personal information that put the females' lives in danger. Just because you cannot see an online aggressor or stalker does not mean you are safe. Always report bullying, name-calling, threats and/or threatening and violent language to the authorities. Always document, get screenshots, and record (if possible) all threats, and never engage with the predator(s).

In the world of predators, even seemingly geeky and harmless gamers or cyber friends, silence equals acceptance and you should never accept victimization.

---

10. *http://www.notinthekitchenanymore.com/*

5

ASSAULTS IN PUBLIC
Real Scenarios

The following are real scenarios that must be presented so that we – together – can dissect what happened, how each scenario might have been handled differently, and how the aggressor sees himself in each scenario.

Scenario 1: Unwanted Advances or Assaults in Public

A girl's track and field coach comments on your appearance. At first, it seems like a compliment, but then it just feels a little weird. At first, the comments are about your hair and clothing, then how you "fill out" your uniform. At some point, he also begins to playfully kick you in the rear end as you run by. He's always laughing about it, but it begins to feel like he's singled you out from the rest of the team. Finally, one day as you run by, he swats you on the bottom with a clipboard he is holding.

Let's stop right here.

You're wondering how this is *assault*.

Sexual assault is an unwanted advance, a touch, that makes a person feel uncomfortable and/or powerless.

When the coach begins inappropriately talking about your appearance, this is sexual harassment (which we will discuss shortly), but even something as seemingly innocent as a kick or swat to the bottom is assault. And let's be clear: There was nothing innocent about this coach's kicks and swats.

In this real-life scenario, the aggressor was a university track coach who only got in trouble after several other athletes on the team and one of the athletes' parents lodged complaints against his behaviors to the university. The athlete on the receiving end of this coach's unwanted attention and affections actually withdrew from the university, giving up her scholarship to run for another university rather than confront her aggressor.

In this particular situation, the female athlete was so stunned and embarrassed, she fell mute. This is (as we will later discuss) an extremely common reaction. In fact, there is actual science behind the reaction of inaction. Females tend to be *retractive*, that is, they tend to shrink away from such situations that are unpleasant and/or need confrontation. Later, this athlete told investigators from the university (which she left) that she didn't want to bring any more attention to herself. For her, it was easier to leave her team, friends, scholarship, and education and transfer to another university than deal with any fallout.

She did nothing wrong, yet she was punished by losing everything.

The aggressor knew his prey. He knew that these "compliments" and "little kicks and swats" would render her shy and helpless. He knew that by taking advantage of a public situation, she would be too embarrassed to say or do anything. He was right.

Predators choose their victims for a reason.

In this case, the aggressor was also supremely confident that his status and position with the university allowed him to behave as such.

WHAT SHOULD SHE HAVE DONE?

Saying, "I don't like that!" would have brought immediate attention to the situation. Those simple words would have told her teammates that she was uncomfortable with being singled out but also let the coach know she was not going to tolerate this unwanted attention any longer. Further, the coach's behavior would have been brought to everyone's attention.

This brings about a very dramatic shift in power.

Repeat: A dramatic shift in power.

In this particular situation, the athlete was afraid that speaking out would cost her placement with the team but, in making it public, any punishment would have been noted by the entire team. Instead, she lost everything by transferring. One month later, when the coach turned his attention to a new victim, complaints to the university followed and he was ultimately fired.

It is important to note that the aggressor, in this case the coach, always moves on to a new target. Aggressive behaviors are never about the victim; aggressive behaviors are about power.

WHAT WOULD YOU DO?

Historically speaking, the predator, i.e., the person in authority, has typically stayed in power despite complaints of his abuse. Thankfully, times are changing; but the burden of proof has always been on the victim, which is why so many stay mute or walk away altogether.

But could you stay?

Would you be willing to lose your position on a team for this coach? Would you be willing to change schools, friends, and your risk your education in this scenario?

These are very real questions you need to ask yourself.

SCENARIO 2: UNWANTED ADVANCES OR ASSAULTS IN PUBLIC

You are among your classmates at school when your history teacher calls you up to his desk. Standing at his desk to go over a grade, the teacher begins rubbing a hand over your shoulders and, moments later, wraps his arm around your waist. While it is hard to imagine that someone would do something so egregious or inappropriate with so many people around, he does. You feel confused. There must be some kind of misunderstanding. Yet, with these feelings of confusion or uncertainty, no one reacts. In this instance, the predator yields the power.

In this real-life situation, multiple teenagers at a high school allegedly complained about inappropriate touching from this same teacher. When complaints were made to administration, the history teacher easily explained everything away, responding that there was no need to worry as he was just a *touchy* person.

This is a typical powerplay by an aggressor who pretends that his actions are innocent by deflecting all concerns: *You're taking it the wrong way; I've always been this way.*

The *I'm-not-worried-about-it-so-you-shouldn't-worry-either* game made the teenagers uncertain about the aggressor's actions. They knew they did not like what just happened but was it morally wrong or illegal?

In this real-life scenario, the complaint made against the teacher had also been privately recorded on another student's phone. When nothing was done about this most recent complaint, the video was put online.

WHAT THEY SHOULD HAVE DONE

When a person or persons of authority refuse to investigate a complaint, gather evidence. In this case, public outcry upon seeing the actual video of a school teacher inappropriately touching a minor was more than anyone could ignore and the teacher was suspended without pay for further inquiry. This is a great example of other people standing up to a predator but, like the previous story, another example of how difficult it is for the victim to speak up.

WHAT SHE SHOULD HAVE DONE

It is important to remember that the girl did absolutely nothing wrong. She is the victim of a predator who took advantage of his authoritative position as her teacher. In an ideal world, however, had she had the training to speak up, she might have said, "Please don't touch me like that." Finding the courage to speak just loudly enough to be heard by only a handful of her peers would have shifted the power significantly.

WHAT WOULD YOU DO?

It is easy to sit where you are now and imagine how bravely you would have spoken out. The reality is most do not. As the seconds tick by with you wondering, *'Is he really touching me?' 'Is that okay?'* and *'I don't like this,'* it then is suddenly too late to say anything.

Maybe I'm overreacting.

Would you have been able to say anything? Or would you simply have moved away from the teacher, out of his reach, and told a counselor or parent about the incident later?

How do I know if this is really wrong? Maybe it's not that big of a deal.

When you feel uncomfortable by an unwanted touch, it is wrong. If you're still uncertain, remember that teachers and coaches are required to take classes that are explicit about inappropriate touching. Teachers and coaches have training on the topic of *not* touching students inappropriately, so if a coach's hand rubs up and down your backside, this goes against all of his or her training. This is a red flag and something you need to talk about. Ask yourself, What would your parent or school principal say about this kind of touching?

SCENARIO 3: UNWANTED ADVANCES OR ASSAULT IN PUBLIC

Was it assault? What was that? It is actually harassment which is a form of assault.

Quite often a person is the victim of assault yet cannot quite wrap her/his mind around what just happened until much, much later. The incident can happen so quickly that the victim is left confused about what actually occurred.

Imagine that you are working as a waitress/waiter, picking up extra hours, as Happy Hour looms. A group of business professionals come in, ordering so much food and drinks that you are most certainly guaranteed a very large tip. The longer they stay (and the bigger the tab grows), however, the more obnoxious one big spender becomes, saying inappropriate things that make you uncomfortable.

In this real-life scenario, a female server was called over to a patron who indicated that he needed to whisper something in her ear. In the restaurant business, it is not uncommon for one person at a table to secretly request to pay the entire tab or bill and, so, the server leaned forward. Instead, the man who appeared to be the leader of the group waited until she was close to him, looked her up and down, and loudly asked how big the tip needed to be for her to come home with him. Remarkably, he then turned to a female coworker to ask, "Should I sleep with her?"

WHAT SHOULD SHE HAVE DONE?

Because he never touched her and, for that matter, because he never actually touched anyone in front of her, she was not sure what to do or how to respond. Instead, as was the aggressor's intention, she was mute, as was his female co-worker. This passive listening (no judgement against the woman who was, clearly, too stunned to react) is very exciting to the aggressor. Having a female audience listen to him discuss how to degrade and demoralize another female is classic predatory behavior. Degrading the waitress but also having another woman, a coworker, involved, was empowering to the predator.

A stunning 90% of U.S. female restaurant workers have experienced some kind of sexual harassment and/or assault in their career. Worse, more than half revealed that this aggression or harassment occurred weekly and that two-thirds reported that it was their manager, supervisor or the restaurant owner who abused them.[1]

It is no surprise, then, that this verbal harassment was not new to this waitress but involving another female (the predator's coworker) "was a first."[2]

What would have been empowering to both of the women at the table (especially the waitress) and a de-masking of the monster seated with his coworkers would have been to ask loudly, "Are you seriously asking her if you should sleep with me? Do you actually think you even have that choice?" All conversation would have stopped and the spotlight would have been placed on him – the monster. Even if he made a joke of it, claimed he had been misunderstood or appeared aghast that she could say such a thing, everyone at the table would forever remember that moment. These are not only potential witnesses to bad behavior for years to come but she would have alerted every woman (and man) at the table to the aggressor's true intentions.

But let's double back to a term you just read – passive listening. What is that?

Passive Listening is listening without reacting. It means to listen without interrupting, not doing anything else while listening. If you're telling a story, lecturing, teaching or coaching, this kind of captive audience is excellent; but in the world of self-defense, passive listening is dangerous. If you hear a person being sexually harassed, bullied, threatened or targeted in any negative (and potentially dangerous) manner yet say nothing, you are both empowering the predator and belittling the victim. Passive listening in the world of self-defense is acceptance.

There is a new saying: *Silence is compliance.*

What does that mean?

---

1. *https://chapters.rocunited.org/2014/10/new-report-90-female-restaurant-workers-experience-sexual-harassment/*

2. *https://www.vice.com/en_us/article/ypa7xv/sexual-harassment-in-waitressing-is-much-uglier-than-you-think*

By doing nothing, by saying nothing, many have argued this is a green-light, an "okay" for what is happening when a person is harassed, stalked, bullied and/or assaulted.

Of course, this is not true but if you see harm being done to another person and do nothing about it, the unspoken message is that it [harm to another person] is okay.

WHAT WOULD YOU HAVE DONE?

In the previous scenarios, a coach, teacher, and businessman were used as examples of predators, but an aggressor can also be a friend, an uncle, a neighbor, a pastor, or even (yes, this happens) a boyfriend.

Understand this: This behavior does not and should never get a "boys will be boys" pass. This is predatory, unacceptable, dangerous behavior. This is demoralizing to all females involved. This is the behavior of a man who does not deem any female involved worthy of consideration beyond gratifying his own fantasy.

In the opening chapter, you were asked to describe what your "bad guy" looks like. Because your neighbor, employer, business partner, coach, friend, or fellow student most likely does not look like a "bad guy," you understand why so many girls and women feel both betrayed and confused by the aggressor in these scenarios.

He seemed like such a nice guy.

Why would he do that to me?

Why didn't I say something?

I thought I could trust him.

These are common responses to the all-too common occurrences of bad behaviors by bad men who just didn't look the part. So, it is time for you to take care of *you*.

We have defined "bad guy." A bad guy can be a stranger or someone you know.

A bad guy does not necessarily have a look; he has an agenda. The bad guy has a behavior. He dismisses and belittles his victims. He is opportunistic, using a public setting and your uncertainty to his advantage, but you can trump your bad guy by adopting new behaviors of your own.

DEFINE SELF-ESTEEM.

What does self-esteem mean to you?

DEFINE STRONG.

What does the word strong mean to you?

DEFINE CONFIDENT.

Are you confident? In what way?

Are you confident in how you move, how you walk or talk?

Having confidence in your appearance is certainly an empowering feeling, but this will not save your life. You need to also have confidence in your own voice. You need to have confidence in your abilities to speak up for yourself and defend your own honor.

Do you have these things in your self-defense armor?

Read on.

6

SHE WAS ASKING FOR IT!

How often is a victim assaulted and then villainized? If a predator could write a plan on how to get away with assaulting people, top on his list would be victim-blaming. As long as we continue this outdated and very dangerous pattern, bad guys will walk.

In the news when we read about a very public assault of a woman by a well-known man, focus is typically put on the woman. *How did she dress? How did she act? Was she after money?*

The harsh reality is girls and women have all too often been blamed for their own assaults. It is yet another reason why so many girls and women do not want to report sexual harassment or sexual assault. They do not want to face very public and harsh scrutiny for simply being a victim.

Just as we can no longer hold onto the notion of what a bad guy looks like, we must change the way we see a victim.

When asked to describe a "victim," during one of my seminars, a high school group depicted a victim as "frail," "weak," "old" and — across the board for all male participants — "female." Of the female respondents, 60% also envisioned a female as a victim. When the word "sexual" was attached to the word "victim," descriptions changed to include a female who is "young," "pretty," "sweet," and "helpless."

WHAT IS A VICTIM?

1. A victim is a person hurt or killed by someone or something by means of crime, accident, disaster, or disease.

2. A victim is a person (or animal) adversely affected by an action or circumstance.

3. A victim is someone duped, tricked, exploited.

Victims are not gender specific. In fact, about 78% all homicide victims are male. Males are most often the victims of violent crimes, except for domestic and sex-related homicides. Those dubious numbers belong to females: Some 45% of female homicide victims are killed by an intimate partner. And black females are four times more likely than white women to be killed by an intimate partner. Those living at poverty level (household incomes less than $12,000) have much higher instances of becoming victims of a violent crime, and senior citizens are rapidly becoming the most targeted victims of online identity theft and mail fraud.[1]

So, what does a victim look like? We see that, in self-defense, our victims are predominantly female (though the numbers of males being the victims of assault by partners or family members are on the rise). Despite what you see in the movies, the female is not always the human Barbie doll running on stilettos. Because predators are opportunists, they are more interested in finding a victim who is accessible and will not fight. Despite what the romance novels and movies suggest, victims of sexual assault come in all shapes and sizes, ages, demographics, and economic status. Just as we cannot draw a picture of a bad guy, there is not a specific image of a victim.

IN SELF-DEFENSE, THERE ARE TWO KINDS OF VICTIMS:

1. Victim of a stranger
2. Victim of a known associate like a family member, friend, neighbor, teacher, classmate, friend of a friend, employer/employee, etc.

SCENARIO 4: IS THIS MY FAULT?

You have been given the exciting opportunity to interview for a dream job, or intern with a well-known professor, or possibly join a dance squad. Upon meeting the person in power, you put out a hand to introduce yourself when he takes it, pulls you in, and gives you a kiss on the cheek or even mouth. The grip on the hand is a little too hard and the hold is a little too long. Never mind – he just kissed you! You are stunned and embarrassed as you almost fell into him. He laughs at your clumsiness and you are instantly awkward and apologetic.

In this real-life scenario, a woman was allegedly greeted by a business mogul outside his private elevator. He took her hand for the shake but did

---

1. *https://www.bjs.gov/index.cfm?ty=tp&tid=92*

not let it go. Then, he pulled her in for a kiss on the cheek and mouth, leaving her feeling "insignificant that he would do that." In real life, however, she said nothing. She simply attempted to laugh it off.

WHAT SHOULD SHE HAVE DONE?

There can be no victim blaming here. Perhaps the woman needed this job opportunity to keep her home, pay medical bills, or pay off a loan. Who knows? Perhaps she was simply so shocked, she couldn't process how wrong this was until much later. This is also a typical response from assault victims.

The best response, however, would have been to end the meeting. There is no possible way her assailant would ever give proper respect to her following this encounter and, most likely, the assaults would continue.

WHAT WOULD YOU DO?

Let's come back to this. Read on.

SCENARIO 5: IS THIS MY FAULT?

You made the soccer team. You made the final cut in a casting call. You got a call back for a second interview for a great job. Whatever the scenario, becoming a victim is the very last thing on your mind. The only thing you care about and are thinking about is your competition or employment opportunity. And then it happens... You feel the eyes of your assailant looking you up and down in a way that is not flattering, professional, appropriate, or respectful. You feel yourself being appraised for your physical assets and you are revolted.

In this real-life scenario, women from the Miss USA pageant were told they would be personally inspected by a high-profile celebrity-type. Reportedly, he would step in front of each contestant and look her up and down for inspection pre-contest. One contestant described it as "the dirtiest I've ever felt in my entire life," and she was left feeling demoralized, like "a piece of meat."[2]

---

2. Blakely, Rhys, "It Was the Dirtiest I Ever Felt," The Times. December 12, 2017. https://www.thetimes.co.uk/article/it-was-the-dirtiest-i-ever-felt-three-women-accuse-trump-of-sex-abuse-60rwwg780

This behavior was not approved by the pageant and there was no such protocol as a pre-contest assessment. This was strictly predatory.

WHAT SHOULD SHE HAVE DONE?

Victim Blaming Alert! For many, the first response to the beauty contestant being ogled is to say, *This is what she asked for. Isn't this what a beauty pageant is about?* Answer: No. While true, the contest is about being judged on beauty, it is not about allowing a non-judge to line up *his* chattel, standing entirely too close to the women for an inspection they already passed by being accepted into the contest.

But now comes the question of what she and the rest of her competitors should have done. The situation is complicated by the fact that it was a beauty contest that measures one's worth by a beauty standard to be judged by others. While pageants offer many scholarships and great opportunities, it can be a slippery and dangerous slope in terms of self-worth, self-esteem and value as a person. There must be standards and safety precautions set in place that are followed, never deviating from what is acceptable treatment and what is not. In this scenario, media exposure and complaints to sponsors of the event can help protect contestants from abuse within the pageant. The fact that this behavior continued so long proves only that no one was willing to speak out against the "authority" of this person in power.

WHAT WOULD YOU HAVE DONE?

Rather than judge the girls and women in this scenario for being in a beauty contest, truly imagine how you would have reacted as the true issue here is what would you do in a scenario in which you feel violated by the person in power? Would you be willing to risk losing the entire competition by complaining out loud or even walking out? Or, as the others did, would you remain quiet and just wait for the disgusting man to go away?

SCENARIO 6: IS THIS MY FAULT?

Following in your grandfather's footsteps, you are accepted into a prestigious military academy. You are a role model; a pioneer. As one of the few female military cadets, you are on top of the world. That is, until you are assaulted by a fellow cadet. In this real-life scenario, the female cadet did not immediately report the assault. In fact, it was another cadet who reported it, blaming the female for "having sex in barracks." Forced, then, to tell what had happened, she was immediately treated as 'the bad guy.'

Despite the fact that a high-ranking decorated soldier from the academy disclosed files that the accused cadet had "documented honor code and behavior violations, negative observation reports, and below-average performance," the predator remained in *good* standing with the military institute while the victim was forced to leave.

In this real-life scenario, the young female cadet was one of 78 other victims to report a sexual assault in a short span of four years, with one former cadet suing the academy for its perpetuation of a "sexually aggressive culture."[3] To date, this young woman still asks what she could have done differently. She would have remained mute had it not been for another person reporting the incident.

WHAT SHOULD SHE HAVE DONE?

Of course, it would have been ideal had she immediately gone to her superiors at the institute to file a report and also allow for a sexual assault forensic exam to be conducted. Although there are countless stories of not being believed, the end result is always the same: the story comes out and people ask, *"Well, if it's true, why didn't she report it?"*

The reality is that the military authorities in this case may have tried to dismiss her allegations, but had she demanded a sexual assault forensic exam, they would not have been able to dismiss the findings. The reality is that there is nothing/no one more valuable than you. Ask yourself this: Had someone broken into your home or dorm room and stolen your personal property, would you have immediately reported this? If someone smashed into your parked car, then quickly drove away, giving you only a glimpse of the license plate, would you have still called the police and notified your insurance company? You would have. So why not speak up for the most valuable thing you own, yourself? Why not, then, call the police and go to a hospital for a rape kit? Even if you are not yet ready to talk to the police, the rape kit will preserve the physical evidence from your assault.

---

3. https://www.thedailybeast.com/cadet-run-out-of-west-point-after-accusing-armys-star-quarterback-of-rape

LET'S PAUSE HERE

WHAT IS A SEXUAL ASSAULT FORENSIC EXAM, OTHERWISE KNOWN AS A RAPE KIT EXAM?

During a rape kit exam, a doctor or nurse who is trained to collect evidence from an assault (as evidence for police) will examine you, giving you a full-body examination. They may take samples (blood, hair, etc.), and they may take pictures of your injuries.

Perhaps evidence from a rape kit would and could have changed how both the cadet victim and predator were treated. Although the legal system is far from perfect, rape kits have played and are continuing to play a huge role in the prosecution of rapists.

But back to the cadets: In this particular situation, the military has had such a long and tarnished history of dismissing female victims that the Defense Department recently instituted more stringent training programs to help prevent sexual assault and harassment, including surveys for members of the armed forces to report incidents, an anonymous help line, and procedures for reducing retaliation against victims.[4] Change comes slowly, but it is coming.

Even if you are afraid of how people will respond, afraid you might lose your job, afraid your family and friends might not believe you, you must defend yourself. If not you, who? A rape kit examination is validation, but it also brings about medical attention should you need it. *Awareness is Armor* is not just words on pages but a call for action for you to protect and defend yourself.

CIRCLING BACK: WHAT SHOULD SHE HAVE DONE IN SCENARIO 4?

In the far more private scenario of the elevator, had the woman pulled back and said, "What do you think you're doing?" the aggressor would have most likely laughed it off or, more probably, left her standing at the elevator – no job opportunity, no money. Witnesses complicate deniability. Without witnesses, the incident becomes one person's word against another. Staying mute, however, cannot be the answer. Additionally, in the case of the cadet, silence never changes anything.

---

4. *https://www.apa.org/monitor/2018/02/sexual-harassment*

As you read, there are dozens (if not more) of current cases of assault in the military, but each new case and each new complaint makes it more difficult for the military to ignore.

There is no judgment here, only facts.

For those who did not speak up for themselves, we understand. It is frightening. It is demoralizing. Speaking up does not guarantee results, but it could pave the way for another victim.

emember this: A person in authority who uses his position to assault another person does not have empathy for his victim. He will do it again and, you can bet, has done it many times before.

WHAT WOULD YOU DO?

Truly imagine these different scenarios and answer honestly: Would you be able to file a report against a popular coach, teacher, or fellow student if you were certain that most, if not all, of the school would be angry with you?

Would you be able to hold your head up, knowing that you were telling the truth even as others were calling you a liar or worse?

Would it be easier to just pretend like nothing happen and let your attacker go?

Re-Define Victim

Re-define Self-Worth

SCENARIO 7: WHEN THE ATTACKER IS CAUGHT AND VICTIM IS STILL ATTACKED

On October 9, 2013, 14-year old Abby Hernandez disappeared while walking home from school. Typically, she would have taken the bus home but, on this day, she decided to walk. Her new boots, however, quickly created painful blisters on her feet so when a "regular looking" guy pulled over to offer a ride, Abby accepted. She knew better, but her feet *were killing her*. She had been taught not to accept rides from strangers, but *he looked like a nice person*.

In this story, there is no need to explain "What Should She Have Done." Even as she stepped into the car, Abby knew it was a mistake. She did as so many others have and *hoped* it would be okay.

The *nice person* hit her with a stun gun, handcuffed her, then drove her 30 miles from her home and held her captive. For nine months, she was tortured, repeatedly raped and demoralized, but she had also learned how to develop a friendship and connect with her captor. This is probably why she is alive today and was ultimately released by her captor. While her story is worth reading (or watching: check out "20/20: Abby Hernandez"), two immediate points must be made:

1. Abby strategized. She never gave up hope. Her instinct for survival was strong. "I remember thinking to myself, 'Okay, I got to work with this guy.' I said [to him], 'I don't judge you for this.'"[5] She found ways to become real to her captor. She wasn't just his victim. She bonded with him. Early on, he made her write a 'runaway' note to her mother in hopes of making the police and volunteer teams stop their search for her. Abby wrote a note but then scratched "help" and "kidnapped" with her fingernail on the paper. Her captor, however, discovered her effort and punished her for it. A second letter was then mailed to her mother, simply saying she was "sorry" but alive.

2. The victim blaming was immediate. When news broke that a letter had arrived and Abby was 'just' a runaway, hateful words began to appear online and in her hometown. Nine months later, when Abby was finally released and her story was revealed, there were many who were still too stubborn, hateful, or ignorant to let go of their previous opinions and continued to berate Abby, posting statements like, "Not buying it. #SorryNotSorry," "I don't think she was held captive at all," and "Victims don't act like that."

Victims don't act like what?

The general public had very limited information about what happened and of the torture Abby endured and of how clever she had been in working with her captor, yet a minority of haters felt the need to diminish a horrendous experience they knew nothing about. Despite photos of her imprisonment and the arrest of her captor, the victim-blaming continued. Essentially, like so many rape victims in our society, she was victimized again.

---

5. *https://abcnews.go.com/US/kidnapping-survivor-abby-hernandez-reveals-stayed-alive-captivity/story?id=57651942*

WHAT WOULD YOU HAVE DONE?

Here it is. Each and every time a high-profile sexual assault case is brought before the public, scrutiny is instantly placed up the victim. Yet when a victim does come out with their story of abuse from decades or mere months ago, they are questioned as to why it *took so long* to report the assault. Those who question the legitimacy of an assault almost always answer their own question: *Because no one will believe you.*

In this case, there is no disputing what happened to Abby yet it was.

Truly imagine yourself in this scenario. How would it feel to survive such a traumatic ordeal only to have people, many from your own town or neighborhood, publicly belittling your experience and calling you a liar? Would you collapse from the scrutiny, go into your room and never come? Would you take to Twitter and fight back?

What victims do and should do are often two very different things.

In this case, fighting on social media with strangers is neither helpful or therapeutic. Nor is hiding in your room.

THE CASE OF ELIZABETH SMART

On June 5, 2002, 14-year-old Elizabeth Smart was abducted by knifepoint in the middle of the night by Brian David Mitchell, a man who had been hired by the family to do repairs to the Smart home. Mitchell and his wife, Wanda Barzee, held her for nine months, repeatedly threatening and raping her. Her story made international news and was on an America's Most Wanted episode that led to her rescue in March of 2003. Her family instantly shielded Elizabeth from the public, only stating that Elizabeth was fine, would not speak of the incident or seek counseling. The news was shocking to therapist and psychologists, such as Ronald Levine, PhD, who said, "Elizabeth Smart has been through an ordeal no one should suffer, let alone an adolescent. Patty Hearst was an adult when she was abducted and it took her years to get over her experience. Elizabeth has had her innocence shattered and her sense of self battered. She will need years of love and undoubtedly competent and caring professional help to ensure her complete recovery."

Preventing Elizabeth from speaking about the incident, like other victims who tried to keep their abuse secret, periodic lapses of depression, anxiety, anger, or anti-social behaviors are common. Victims who refuse to acknowledge their abuse can often be triggered, re-living the assault, by a sound, scents, and/or visual stimulation, leading to more regression and anxiety.[6]

An assault is not only about the victim but his or her entire family.

In fact, it would take eight years before her captors would be brought before a court as Mitchell's lawyers argued that their client was mentally unfit to stand trial. On October 1, 2009, Elizabeth took the stand and testified before a judge, jury, her captor and family, giving details she had never before shared. Following her testimony, her father, Ed Smart, tearfully admitted that his daughter said things he had never heard. Elizabeth had buried her torment and torture for eight years.

"I had no idea what she had gone through."[7]

Realizing, at last, how much she needed to speak out, it was her father who broke the family's silence and urged Elizabeth to write a book about her experience and speak publicly.

"I wanted to leave it all in the past and didn't want to have it brought up in daily conversation," she said. "I didn't want anyone to know what had happened. It was the worst nine months of my life. For years, I didn't write about it, didn't want to think about it."[8]

It was speaking before a packed courtroom, confronting her abuser but also including her family in her abuse that ultimately gave her her life back.

She need not justify herself or her feelings to other people. Healing came from speaking up and caring for herself (at last) and her family.

Don't wait seven years!

WHAT SHE DID DO AND SO CAN YOU

Your truth is your own. If you do not defend yourself, who will? For Abby, most of her haters have been shut down but, beautifully, Abby doesn't care. She knows her truth, she knows her worth, and she's more appreciative of life than ever before.

---

6. Allen, Colin, "Therapists React to the Elizabeth Smart Case: The Real Challenge Starts Now for Elizabeth and Her Family." *Psychology Today*, March 1, 2003.

7. CBS News, "Elizabeth Smart's Testimony." October 1, 2009. *https://www.youtube.com/watch?v=e0lBXfcxCV0*

8. Lords, Christina, "For Years Elizabeth Smart Didn't Tell Her Story," *Idaho Statesman.* April 4, 2018.

Abby speaks about her abuse and did so almost immediately, caring for herself, her mother and new, growing family.

You cannot care about what others think. It is your life. It is your story. It is your road to wellness, self-esteem, and happiness.

7

TAYLOR SWIFT DID SOMETHING ABOUT IT

That's right. Taylor Swift. The popstar. The wholesome, former country singer-songwriter, the goody two-shoes, the role model parents loved that their preteens loved. *That* Taylor Swift. She was victimized. She wasn't asking for it; she wasn't looking for trouble. When it happened, however, she initially froze. Like so many other victims, she was so surprised it took her a moment to compartmentalize what had just happened and, for that, as you will read, she would be questioned.

But, first, another scenario to consider:

SCENARIO 8: IS THIS MY FAULT?

Despite being in a public setting, someone grabs and squeezes your buttocks. You are standing in a crowded room, on a bus or at a train station; you are with a group of friends or about to walk out on to a stage to present a project you have been working on for some time when it happens. This is an assault. Someone grabbing and squeezing your bottom is a sexual advance and an assault upon your person.

In this real-life scenario, an NBC reporter, Alex Bozarjian, covering a live broadcast of a race, was speaking to the camera when a man, broke away from the pack of other runners and slapped, then grabbed her buttocks. The reporter was so stunned that she stopped talking for a moment before she could regain her composure. As a professional, she finished the segment but it wasn't easy. The act of aggression was so fast she had to wonder if it had actually happened except that she could still feel the sting from the slap.

WHAT SHOULD SHE HAVE DONE?

The video (on YouTube under "Who's the Man Who Slapped Reporter Live on Air?") had millions of views within just weeks of the assault and

47

while the overwhelming majority supported the 23-year-old reporter, there were others who told her to "get over it," "stop being a brat," and "he [assailant] was just caught up in the moment," to which Bozarjian stated, "It's not okay for you to help yourself to a woman's body just because you feel like it."

While her assailant made the classic public appeal: *It was an awful act* and *I am not that kind of person that people are portraying me as*, his words changed nothing. This youth minister and Boy Scouts of America leader felt compelled to assault a young woman because it seemed fun and funny. This is not the first time a female reporter has been goosed, slapped, assaulted on live TV. When Sue Turton, reporting live from the streets of Oxford, was pinched, Turton considered filing a complaint but the outrage in protest for the assailant was so powerful that Turton let it go, sending a strong message of its own. Once again, there is no blame being cast upon Turton, who is already a victim of assault. By bending to public demand in a culture that allows women to be objectified, she felt doubly victimized.[1]

Bozarjian, however, had a message of her own. "I think in order to make any kind of change you have to be a little bit drastic. And you have to, kind of, chip away at this toxic culture that permeates our society." So, she filed a police report.[2]

WHAT WOULD YOU HAVE DONE?

Seriously? What would you have done if just as many fans or viewers wrote in to your TV station or found you on Facebook, Twitter, Instagram and berated you for "being a baby."

Would you have filed a police report? Would you have stood your ground? Or would public pressure have gotten to you?

How would you feel if a Youth Minister/Boy Scout Leader plead his innocence to the world and begged you to forgive him because he wasn't "that kind of person?"

Each time we shrug off an assault, we reinforce the notion that unwanted touches are okay. Each time we passively listen or watch an assault, we are condoning violence against victims.

---

1. *https://www.theguardian.com/media/2007/jul/31/broadcasting.channel41*

2. *https://www.wsav.com/news/local-news/wsavs-alex-bozarjian-addresses-bridge-run-incident/*

But wait! Is a pinch, a goose, a slap really sexual assault?

Let's review: *What is assault vs. harassment?*

WHAT IS SEXUAL HARASSMENT?

According to the U.S. Government and the U.S. Equal Employment Opportunity Commission, sexual harassment is:

It is unlawful to harass a person (an applicant or employee) because of that person's sex. Harassment can include "sexual harassment" or unwelcome sexual advances, requests for sexual favors, and other verbal or physical harassment of a sexual nature.

Harassment does not have to be of a sexual nature, however, and can include offensive remarks about a person's sex. For example, it is illegal to harass a woman by making offensive comments about women in general.

Both victim and the harasser can be either a woman or a man, and the victim and harasser can be the same sex.

Although the law doesn't prohibit simple teasing, offhand comments, or isolated incidents that are not very serious, harassment is illegal when it is so frequent or severe that it creates a hostile or offensive work environment or when it results in an adverse employment decision (such as the victim being fired or demoted).

The harasser can be the victim's supervisor, a supervisor in another area, a co-worker, or someone who is not an employee of the employer, such as a client or customer.

This legal statute does not change when we are talking about elementary, middle- or high school, or college students with a high school teacher, administrator, coach or another student. It does not change if we're talking about a neighbor, a music or art teacher, the postal delivery man or a friend.

While sexual assault, which includes rape and/or groping, grabbing, is part of sexual harassment, it also includes a hostile environment where constant jokes, suggestions, lured looks or gestures are made to degrade, embarrass or humiliate another person. Here's a hint: If the accused later attempts to dismiss these actions with the explanation of it just being "locker room talk," its most likely sexual harassment. The more we dismiss sexual harassment as 'oh, its just locker room talk,' the more we normalize bad behaviors.

WHAT IS SEXUAL ASSAULT?

By definition from the United States Department of Justice, any type of sexual contact or *behavior* that occurs without the *explicit consent* of the recipient is sexual assault.

But if you're still in need of another scenario, look no further than the next scenario.

SCENARIO 9: HAND UP THE SKIRT

It was during a preconcert photo opportunity in 2013 that two radio DJs posed with Taylor Swift when DJ David Mueller put his hand up under Swift's skirt and squeezed. In a photo obtained by TMZ, a tabloid news website, the image very clearly hows Swift moving away from his grasp and Mueller's hand placed below her buttocks.[3] Witnesses, including Swift's mother and her personal bodyguard, saw the singer visibly jump, then lean away from Mueller and into the female DJ's side. Here's where the story of a superstar is actually quite common.

WHAT SHOULD HAVE TAYLOR DONE?

She should have screamed, "Get your hands off of me!" She should have screamed, "Assault!" But Taylor, like millions of other victims [no judgement] was so stunned by this unwanted sexual contact and sexual behavior that she fell mute.

When finally allowed to process what had happened, she told her mother and here is where the story continues to be very typical.

Her mother, Andrea Swift, reacted like a typical mother. *How would this define Taylor?* she wondered. Because of Taylor's celebrity, Andrea had other worries as well. "I did not want her to have to live through the endless memes and gifs that tabloid media and internet trolls decided to come up with - doctoring the pictures… and making her relive this awful moment over and over again," she said.[4]

In fact, so concerned about her own daughter's welfare, Andrea had wanted to keep the assault "discreet and quiet and confidential." This is a typical response. *Please make this go away.* So, the Swifts quietly filed a grievance with the owner of the radio station whereupon Mueller was

3. *https://www.tmz.com/2017/08/10/taylor-swift-takes-stand-butt-groping-trial-quotes/*

4. *https://www.bbc.com/news/entertainment-arts-40937429*

fired. Ironically, it would have remained quiet had not Mueller made such a stink.

He brought a lawsuit against Taylor, claiming that she got him fired and sought three million in damages. Taylor countersued for a symbolic dollar. It was not about the money; it was about the principle.

WHAT TAYLOR "LOOK WHAT YOU MADE ME DO" SWIFT DID

This story might have only been a blip in the news had it not been for the dollar. When a lawsuit was brought against the victim, the victim stood up. Mueller's lawsuit, asserting that Taylor had destroyed Mueller's career, was thrown out by the judge which then led the way for Taylor to take the stand in her counter-defense. As she spoke to Mueller's lawyer, Taylor said, "You can ask me a million questions. I'm never going to say anything different. I never have said anything different." When questioned on whether she was critical of her own bodyguard or not stepping forward when he thought Mueller put his hand under the singer's skirt, Taylor didn't hesitate. "I'm critical of your client sticking his hand under my skirt and grabbing my ass." To ensure that the point was not lost, she restated, "He stayed attached to my bare ass-cheek as I lurched away from him. . . He had a handful of my ass." Despite her own sweet-girl reputation, she did not want to sugarcoat what had happened to her.[5]

When Mueller's lawyer suggested that it was Taylor's fault his client had lost his job, Taylor said, "I'm not going to let you or your client make me feel in any way that this is my fault. Here we are years later, and I'm being blamed for the unfortunate events of his life that are the product of his decisions – not mine."[6]

Taylor Swift is, indeed, a role model.

The entire purpose of this book is to empower you through awareness. *Awareness is Armor* is not just being aware of your bad guy, your potential bad guy, but also being aware of your own actions – to prevent you from becoming a victim. The following chapter is *not* about judgement but a reminder of how alcohol, drugs, inattentiveness can increase your odds of becoming a victim of assault. Do not be critical of the victim in this scenario but understand how to better defend yourself at all times.

---

5. *https://www.washingtonpost.com/news/arts-and-entertainment/wp/2017/12/06/taylor-swift-explains-her-blunt-testimony-during-her-sexual-assault-trial/*

6. *https://www.glamour.com/story/taylor-swift-sexual-assault-trial-cross-examination*

8

THE CASE OF "STEEP" PRICE

Scenario #10: The Victim Without Memory

On January 18, 2015, an unidentified woman whom the court named "Emily Doe" attended a fraternity party and drank so much alcohol that she lost consciousness while walking home.

- By her own admission, she drank too much.

- By her own admission, she wishes she had not.

- By her own admission, she does not know how it came to be that she was assaulted.

What happened following her blackout Emily Doe only knows through witnesses and forensic reports. She was so drunk that she did not wake up for many hours after the attack. What is known is that Emily Doe was naked when two graduate students from Stanford University happened by on their bicycles. They saw Brock Turner, a stand-out swimming athlete with Stanford University on top of her, "aggressively thrusting his hips into her," said witness Carl-Fredrick Arndt. "The guy [Brock Turner] stood up, then we saw that she wasn't moving still. So, we called him out on it. And the guy ran away, my friend, Peter [Jonsson], chased after him."

Turner claimed the sex, with Emily Doe lying naked and unconscious on the ground next to a dumpster, was consensual despite the fact that her blood alcohol level was so high that she was rendered comatose for hours. When the case went to court, Turner's lawyer repeatedly urged the jury that "the only one we can believe is Brock, because she doesn't remember." The victim on trial was Brock Turner. Just before his sentencing, Turner's father appealed to the judge in a letter saying, "His [Brock] life will never be the one that he dreamed about and worked so hard to achieve. That is a steep price to pay for 20 minutes out of his 20 plus years of life."

Friends and family members of an aggressor never want to call a rapist a rapist, any more than they want to identify the deed as an assault. For Brock Turner's family, his assault on Emily Doe was "20 minutes out of his 20 plus years of life," just as other aggressors explain that after they were caught (in person or on tape) pinching, kissing, pinning against a wall, grabbing a woman by her genitalia, abusing, coercing, or otherwise assaulting a woman that "that wasn't me. I'm not *that* person."

In turn, the victim spoke out by way of letter to the judge before a sentence was given. While Brock Turner's *tormented* 20 minutes altered his life, Emily Doe wrote [to her assailant]:

"You took away my worth, my privacy, my energy, my time, my safety, my intimacy, my confidence, my own voice, until today. ... I don't want my body anymore. I was terrified of it," she wrote. "My independence, natural joy, gentleness, and steady lifestyle I had been enjoying became distorted beyond recognition. I became closed off, angry, self-deprecating, tired, irritable, empty," she said.

Shortly after, Brock Turner was given a six-month sentence, serving only three months, when the standard punishment would have been up to 10 to 14 years in prison. For many, this wasn't just a case of victim blaming; it was case of entitlement as well. Statistics show that male predators of a lower economic standing are far more likely to be imprisoned while upper-class white males walk or receive a slap on the wrist. Such was the case in the Brock Turner trial.

This case, in and of itself, was not that unusual. Sadly, there have been stories like this and worse throughout history. Women, drunk or sober, at night or in the morning, walking the streets or going for an early morning jog, alone with their thoughts or out with friends have been assaulted. And, then, for reasons that have everything to do with politics, sports, business, religion, prominence or denial, the woman's behaviors are questioned while the assailant(s) walk free. *He's not that kind of guy.* We even have a president who bragged about assaulting women by grabbing their privates, but *he's not that kind of guy.*

---

1. *https://www.cbsnews.com/news/thousands-push-for-judge-in-stanford-sex-assault-case-to-be-removed-brock-turner*

Brock Turner's victim is forever a victim of his actions. *He didn't mean to do it.* But she is forever scarred by his deeds. His 20 minutes is her lifetime.

But it is here that you must define and re-define (again) the word "victim."

Are you a victim?

Will you be a victim?

What have you done to prepare yourself against this probability?

If one in every five American women is assaulted at some point in her life, what are you doing to protect yourself?

Before we talk more about that, it must be stated that Carl-Fredrick Arndt and Peter Jonsson are heroes. They were not passive bystanders who saw an assault but did nothing. They actively chased Brock Turner down. They got medical help for and played a role in bringing some semblance of justice to the victim.

Note: What Brock's family merely called a "steep price" – three months in jail for rape, the 20-minute rape of an unconscious woman by a dumpster — actually took away another person's worth, privacy, time, safety, confidence, independence and joy. But in September 2019, after serving over four years of her own imprisonment, Emily Doe found her voice. She revealed her true identity as Chanel Miller, releasing her book, *Know My Name: A Memoir*, to share both her story and her voice with the world. Welcome back, Chanel!

She is a survivor.

9

IN DEFENSE OF YOUR ODDS

Every 98 seconds, an American is sexually assaulted, yet far too few girls and women take self-defense classes.

Unfortunately, as awful as the story from the previous chapter is, it is a reality check. At least one in every five female college students has been a victim of sexual assault, with freshman and sophomore females at the greatest risk of assault. Most often, the assailants in attempted or completed assaults on college campuses are acquaintances, boyfriends, dates, or classmates of the victim.[1]

Experts believe that the newfound freedom of living without parental control, along with a culture that emboldens fraternities, athletic prowess, and endless partying increases the odds of sexual assault.

Why, then, don't more women take self-defense?

THE TWO DIFFERENT KINDS OF SELF-DEFENSE

- The Lecture – A self-defense lecture is typically a two-to-four-hour presentation conducted by a single speaker or panel of experts from martial arts, law enforcement, public safety professions who, much like this book, offer scenarios, statistics, and strategies for self- and situational awareness, defensive and offensive tactics.

- Hands On – A self-defense class usually takes place in a martial arts dojo (studio), fitness or athletic club setting that allows for proper gear, like mats, padded targets, etc, to be used while learning physical maneuvers for self-defense.

---

1. *https://www.washingtonpost.com/national/health-science/showing-women-how-to-resist-sexual-aggression-reduced-chances-of-rape/2015/06/15/3935ba14-1067-11e5-9726-49d6fa26a8c6_story.html*

THE LECTURE VS. THE CLASSROOM SETTING

Which is better? The answer may surprise you.

A four-hour lecture yields greater results than a two-hour physical class but there is a "but."

True self-defense, truly becoming proactive in defending yourself is more than just learning how to flip or punch a person. Statistically speaking, women who took just one self-defense class where they learned how to punch and kick are at greater risk than those who completed a four-hour lecture. Why?

With the lecture, women are less stressed about simulating attacks and trying to memorize multi-step self-defense moves. In this case, active listening shows that participants are more apt to pay attention, take notes, and think proactively. *When is a better time to go jogging? When I park my car in a parking garage, I will have my coworker/roommate meet me. I'll call campus security to walk me to my dorm. I will never leave my drink unattended.*

By empowering women with practical steps of adjusting schedules, considering where to park a car or exercise, using social media, dating, and knowing when/where to text, for example, the odds of physical threats lessened. It is not enough to train women how to stop an assault once it begins. Women need to become more aware of their surroundings to deter a potential predator from ever launching an assault in the first place.[2] When female college students were taught how to recognize and resist sexual aggression in lectures, a study showed that their chances of being assaulted (raped) over a one-year period was reduced to nearly half.[3] Learning how to identify predatory behaviors and characteristics has proven very empowering in terms of preemptive self-defense.

It cannot be said enough times: *A sexual predator is an opportunist.* Despite what Hollywood loves to sell, most predators care less about what a victim looks like and more about opportunity. An unlocked door, a distracted walker, an all-too trusting neighbor, a drunken party-goer, or a bored teenager online are *opportunities.*

---

2. Brecklin, L, Ullman, S.E., "Self-Defense or Assertiveness Training and Women's Responses to Sexual Attacks." Journal of Interpersonal Violence. 2005 June; Vol. 20 (6): pages 738-62.

3. https://www.washingtonpost.com/national/health-science/showing-women-how-to-resist-sexual-aggression-reduced-chances-of-rape/2015/06/15/3935ba14-1067-11e5-9726-9d6fa26a8c6_story.html

IS THE PHYSICAL SELF-DEFENSE CLASS WORTH IT?

Absolutely. 100%. The lecture is invaluable. That is, a good lecture is invaluable. Great empowerment comes from learning how to handle a situation before it becomes a *situation* (wait until you read the story of Leigh Ann!), but there is also something to be said for knowing that you can throw a solid punch or kick. There is something to be said for knowing *how* to throw a solid punch or kick!

Another reality is that we don't always see the signs of an assault until it is too late. Knowing that you can break a nose, gauge out an eye, or destroy a kneecap (much easier than you think) is very empowering. The key is learning how to find a class that is best suited for you.

Most of us are kinesthetic learners, that is, we learn best when we're actually physically working through a movement or motion. In fact, when girls and women combine lecture and tactical self-defense, they are **98.3% more likely to avoid assaults altogether**.[4] With at least 12 hours of training/education about safety, sexual assault and self-defense, 97% were able to fight off their attacker, and upward of 80% used the power of their voice and body language to thwart an assault.[5] Those statistics speak for themselves.

The perfect combination is taking both a lecture and tactical class annually. True self-defense is never a one-time deal but a life-long, ongoing journey of self-empowerment and growth.

So, again, why don't more women take self-defense classes? For reasons such as "I'm too out of shape," or "It costs too much money," to "I don't need self-defense; I have a gun," and the all too common, "I'm afraid of getting hurt." There is no good reason to ignore your own safety.

Let's talk about why you don't want to learn how to protect yourself.

OH, YOU'RE GOING TO GET HURT

If you are assaulted, you will be hurt.

If you fight back to save your own life, you will be hurt. If you do not fight, the probability of being beaten, punched, or worse is also high. A

---

4. *http://modelmugging.org/self-defense-for-women/*

5. *https://warriorpublications.wordpress.com/2015/06/16/women-trained-to-resist-sexual-assault-far-less-likely-to-be-raped-study/*

sexual assault, without a punch, is violent and terrible. As you read about Emily Doe/Chanel Miller, she was never punched. In fact, she has no memory of the rape at all, yet it took her over four years just to be able to share her name with the world. The emotional pain and agony of her assault was horrific.

Just as you have been asked to define what "victim," "self-esteem," and "bad guy" are in your mind, you need to define "injury" because the long-term effects of rape can be far worse than the average person understands.

It is remarkable how many people think injuries can only come from the sexual assault itself. When they question why a person did not immediately announce to the world that they were a victim of physical, mental, and emotional rape, ("Why didn't you talk about this before?"), they exhibit a lack of understanding about what sexual assault truly is. It is not "20 minutes" of a person's life. It is not one terrible moment, followed by a hospital visit and one police report. It can be years and years of therapy and distrust; years and years of fear combined with emotional and physical scars; years and years of sleep interrupted with nightmares and flashbacks, hearing noises and growing paranoid; years and years of insecurities, self-doubt, guilt and self-loathing. Smells can ignite a painful flashback. The sound of a voice or the certain phrase can undo years of recovery. That *20 minutes* can be that harmful.

Oh, you really can get hurt.

Do not read these statements as a threat or scare-tactic but understand the message as it is intended. Sexual assault is a multi-layered horror show that features real pain and agony with a very real predator and a lingering effect that molds you – in one way or another. Each time the victim of a sexual assault hears of a politician, business mogul or athlete who has assaulted another person (and, worse, walked away without punishment), it is a personal and private hell of reliving her/his own experience. Each time a person asks (born of ignorance) why the victim did not speak up earlier, blame is placed yet again on the victim.

Remember the expression: Silence is Compliance?

This has been used to victim-blame. *She didn't say anything so it must have been okay!*

We KNOW that many victims become so frightened that they are unable to yell or call for help. A victim's silence has been unfairly used against her (or him) throughout history. But we also know that silence can be detrimental to the victim's psyche as well. Long after the crime has been committed, a victim will punish him or herself for not speaking up or yelling.

Do not allow fear of being hurt minimize your survival.

Do not ask, "Will I be hurt?" but tell yourself, "I will survive." This is why you must learn to stand up for yourself – both physically and emotionally.

I'M NOT IN PROPER PHYSICAL CONDITION

For the women who believe they are not in the required physical conditioning to defend themselves and thus do not take a self-defense class, they are already in great jeopardy. As you will later read, this is exactly the kind of mindset a predator looks for. Predators want an easy mark. They need a victim who can be easily bullied, frightened, and directed. *"Shut up or I will hurt you." "Don't move or I will ..."*

Fitness level is important. The stronger you are, the greater your chances of fighting. Predators do not want a prolonged fight on their hands and will often actively choose a weaker victim. Always try to increase your fitness level for a happier, healthier, more active and prolonged life. But never pass up an opportunity for self-defense training because of a lowered fitness level. You deserve to learn how to defend yourself.

I DON'T HAVE THE TIME FOR SELF DEFENSE/I DON'T HAVE THE MONEY FOR SELF DEFENSE

Priority is an amazing thing.

Women sit for hours and spend billions (collectively) on hair, manicures, massages, make-up and specialized procedures but neglect the most important thing – their lives.

In truth, many organizations and businesses charge too much money for self-defense programs. Ideally, this should be a free service. If you look, however, you can find self-defense classes offered by police, local women's organizations and women's groups that are either free or charge only for the materials required in the class. Make it a girls' night out with a group of friends and do this at least twice a year.

IT'S NOT REALISTIC ... IT WON'T WORK

In October 2019, an Internet celebrity stated that 99% of women are "too weak" to fight 99% of men, theorizing that even if a woman knew Brazilian jiu-jitsu, she would not have the size or strength to beat her opponent. On the pretense of looking out for our interests, he suggested that women learning martial arts for self-defense purposes was dangerous as it only set us up for failure.

So confident was Kristopher Zylinski in his beliefs that 99% of women could not properly protect themselves after learning how to fight that he agreed to fight mixed martial artist (MMA) grappler Tara LaRosa, a 41-year-old woman who stood at 5'6" and 134-pounds. Prior to the fight, Zylinski maintained that because he was in good physical condition, his own prowess could dominate a trained female MMA fighter.

Once the match began, it went to the ground quickly and in a matter of minutes, LaRosa forced her male opponent to tap out. Later, in an interview, Zylinski admitted there was little he could do to defend against her assault.[6]

Earlier that same year, a female MMA fighter was assaulted while waiting for an Uber. The predator walked up to Polyana Viana, nicknamed "the Iron Lady" or "Lady of Steel," and asked what time it was. When she told him, "He said, 'Give me your cell phone. Don't try to react because I'm armed.' He was really close to me. So, I thought 'if it's a gun, he won't have time to draw it.' So, I stood up. I threw two punches and a kick. He fell, then I caught him in a rear-naked choke." As Viana restrained her would-be assailant, he actually begged her to call the police because he was afraid she was going to beat him up more. In the image provided by ABC news, Viana caused significant damage to her assailant's face in mere second.[7]

The reality is, there is no guarantee on self-defense but should you learn techniques that teach you how to think and react, what safety measures to consider about how and where to walk and park, how to project yourself as someone not to be trifled with, etc., you are more

---

6. https://www.nydailynews.com/news/national/ny-female-mma-fighter-beats-man-internet-troll-20191029-uiwehrpoafezred2eagwqrkteq-story.html

7. https://www.abc.net.au/news/2019-01-08/polyana-viana-ufc-fighter-beats-up-would-be-robber-in-brazil/10697010?pfmredir=sm

likely to defend yourself. Mental and emotional empowerment are incredible tools in self-defense.

Where and how you train, however, means everything. The self-defense class you sign up for may not be practical or realistic, and it is for this (and other) reasons that this book was created. The reality is, you will not learn how to 'take down' an opponent in one three-hour session class. Most well-meaning and qualified (usually) male instructors teach self-defense to mainstream, everyday women, using techniques that require:

- Years of practice
- Greater strength/height/mobility for leverage
- Multiple steps to execute
- Larger and stronger hands to execute moves

Self-defense for women should be size-friendly. It should be fast, and the techniques should be easy to remember and simple in execution. In a moment of great surprise or shock, you should be able to recall and react with ease. If your great move to break a hand grip uses seven steps to do so … well, that's not realistic. As empowering as the stories of LaRosa and Viana are, these two women have many years of training under their black belts.

It is important to research different self-defense courses and the instructor! Do not be afraid to contact the instructor and ask him/her for their resume, personal background, and how they got into teaching self-defense. Ask for references and check them out!

If the instructor you are talking to tells you that he or she has "fool-proof" techniques that allow you to disable or flip a person, be wary. No technique is fool-proof. As instructors, we can only teach specific moves to students. There is no way to know what the situation will be that may require self-defense, and it is for this reason that your emotional and mental state are far more important than physical prowess.

Ask what kind of defense tactics are taught. Will you learn how to fight if you are on the ground or in a car?

---

8. https://www.washingtonpost.com/technology/2019/12/05/uber-disclosed-sexual-assaults-us-rides-last-year-its-long-awaited-safety-report/?arc404=true

In 2018, more than 3,000 sexual assaults were reported involving Uber.[8] Consider for a moment that these numbers do not even include Lyft. In one year, thousands of victims were assaulted by a driver they hired to safely transport them. As you will later read in Chapter Seventeen, pepper spray, tasers and guns can be used against you. Learning leverage in closed quarters could save your life.

I Don't Need Self-Defense; I Carry a Gun

Congratulations. You just said the #1 thing that causes every self-defense instructor and every victim to roll their eyes.

Understandably, this statement makes people feel better, but now let's talk about the real world.

While many law enforcement and security instructors also make these same ridiculous utterances, they are wrong. In real life, the sexual predator does not announce him (or her) self. In real life, most victims never have time to retrieve a can of mace, a gun, a knife, a baton, or a cell phone to call for help. Most victims never see the attack coming.

There are many rosy depictions of women earning concealed handgun licenses with promises that gun ownership can reduce instances of rape. This is, in fact, wrong and negligent information to pass along to the public.[9] [10] [11]

If the scenario is that a woman is already holding her gun in hand as she watches her aggressor slowly approach, then, yes, having a gun would be a great defense. But how realistic is that? In real life, only 10% of rapes are committed by a complete stranger who the victim never saw coming. In most cases, the women are with a person they trust and their gun is nowhere near them. In most cases, the assault is a blindside attack, leaving no time to do anything but scream unless she is trained to defend herself. But in most cases, because of the suddenness of the assault, because of the shock and the surprise, because of the poor or nonexistent training in preparation of this moment and, as you will later read, because

9. Grimes, David Robert. "Guns Don't Offer Protection" The Guardian. March 25, 2013. https://www.theguardian.com/science/blog/2013/mar/25/guns-protection-national-rifle-association

10. John Hopkins Bloomberg School of Public Health https://www.jhsph.edu/research/centers-and-institutes/johns-hopkins-center-for-gun-policy-and-research/publications/IPV_Guns.pdf

11. Hodnett, Gentry, "Guns & Rape Prevention: A Dangerous Myth". March, 17, 2016. http://ocrcc.org/guns-rape-prevention-a-dangerous-myth/

of the retractive responses of most women, the victim will simply fold, unable to even scream.

I'm being attacked.

I'm going to be killed.

I can't believe this is happening to me.

Forget the gun ruse.

In learning how to defend yourself, you should discover that you already possess very effective and powerful (yes, powerful) weapons. Your elbows, knees and teeth can be vicious, and your head and hands also make good weapons. However, if you've never learned an elbow or heel palm strike, or learned to effectively use your knees or feet, it is hard to believe you can defend yourself. You can. Rest assured, you already have weapons with you at all times. But you must learn to use what you have.

SELF-DEFENSE INSTRUCTION AND SELF-LOVE

You cannot leave your safety to another person. For most victims, their lives are reduced to a single moment in which they must rely upon another person's humanity, civility, decency, and compassion. Can you fathom the horror of looking into the eyes of a monster and, with no ability to save your own life, you can only hope he will have mercy upon your soul?

Some of you can. For this, there can only be gratitude that you survived to read these words and acknowledgment given to the emotional journey of recovery you have travelled. You never asked for this, but you can survive it. Be proud of yourself. You are a survivor.

For those who have never been assaulted in any manner, this is a grace you cannot fully comprehend, and let's hope that fact never changes.

For all, it should be understood that self-defense is synonymous with self-love. You are fighting for yourself. You are protecting yourself. Learning to protect yourself is a never-ending job you should LOVE! You should be as faithful to self-defense training as you are to maintenance for your car, beauty treatments for your person, or checking on financial statements at your bank.

Remember this: Not one victim really thought she would be attacked … and then she was.

10

REACTION AND INACTION

Men are reactive. In times of threat, women (as a stereotypical rule) tend to be inactive. Or retractive. We shrink inward. How often have you seen a male lash out at something that startles him while a female draws her hands inward and screams?

WhetherI am teaching a self-defense seminar for a corporation, a private group or one-on-one, men and women are typically different in their responses. When someone is called from the audience to be the "attacker," there is a nervous giggle from the crowd. The male will ask, "You're not going to hurt me, are you?" Once assured he will not be throat-punched, the male is typically *okay* with then simulating a choke hold. Women, however, will apologize while pathetically choking the "victim"/instructor. It is great comedic relief for the audience, but it is always the same. The female attacker repeatedly whispers, "Sorry!" while playing the role of attacker.

Simply put, most males and females react differently to confrontation. As a general (albeit sweeping) rule, males bow up to confrontation. *What's your problem? You lookin' at me?* Females step back, avert eye contact, and hope to get the heck out of the threatening situation.

The following pages and chapters have been created from years and years of training athletes, students, victims and survivors, both male and female, young and old. ***Awareness is Armor*** was designed to have you think more about you; think more about your surroundings; think more about your personal weapons; think more about how you may be viewed by others; and think more about the value of your life.

SCENARIO 11: AGGRESSOR ACTION/VICTIM INACTION

Note: This title seems to suggest placing blame on the victim. No blame. It is simply a reality you must consider.

You are on an airplane, in an elevator, or in a secluded area that is semi-public when you are assaulted. Though you are in public, you feel trapped.

In this real-life scenario, a woman was sexually harassed on a flight from Phoenix to New York. When she rose to use the bathroom, she was suddenly pushed from behind into the small lavatory and raped. Shockingly, in-flight sexual assaults are on the rise, according the FBI data, since 2016. So much so that a National In-Flight Sexual Misconduct Task Force was created to combat this rise in sexual assaults. Additionally, 68% of flight attendants report being sexually harassed while working.[1]

Experts believe that the intimacy of shared seats and alcohol have led to these assaults. In the case of this particular passenger, the sexual assault began while seated together when the man grabbed and kissed her. Witnesses both heard and saw her push him away and tell him that it "couldn't happen." With so many witnesses around, how could the assault have escalated to rape in a bathroom?

WHAT SHOULD SHE HAVE DONE?

The woman was assaulted while seated but believed with so many people around her and her it "couldn't happen" warning to her assailant that she was then safe. She was not.

What more could she have done?

Without placing blame, what should she have done next?

According to the National In-Flight Sexual Misconduct Task Force, she should have immediately contacted a flight attendant to both report the crime and to request being seated elsewhere. Instead, mistakenly, she went to the bathroom.

---

1. *https://www.star-telegram.com/news/local/crime/article238558198.html*

WHAT WOULD YOU DO?

Although the witnesses to this account did nothing, we hope that today's fellow passengers would step in to help. But don't count on it. All too often, a person needs to hear a "help" before acting. Unfortunately, however, many women are simply too stunned and/or embarrassed to call for help. But our voice is a powerful weapon.

Remember that even in a crowded room, even an airplane, an assault can occur.

You must use your voice!

Predators do *not* want attention drawn to themselves or to their actions. What they want and need is to be in an isolated area so that if you were to fight or yell, no help would be available to you. More on that later.

For the purpose of this section, however, let's pay attention to the predator who has become so confident and so seasoned (or drunk) in how he attacks and who he chooses that he is confident she will not fight back.

For this predator, silence equals cooperation.

Would you be able to shout for help on a crowded airplane?

Are you willing to further anger your aggressive seatmate by pressing the Attendant call button and loudly ask to be reassigned a new seat?

SCENARIO 12: AGGRESSOR ACTION/VICTIM INACTION

This can't be happening. This is my job. This is my sport! You are an athlete among your own teammates when the team's manager grabs you. Not only are your teammates present but so, too, is the manager's own wife. Hardly able to believe what is happening, you do nothing.

Maybe this isn't what I think it is. Maybe I'm misinterpreting this …

In reality, however, you quickly realize this is all too real. In this real-life scenario, a female athlete on a national team was meeting the team manager regarding sponsorship money and an upcoming World Cup competition. His own family and team present, he felt empowered to make a move when the wife was not looking.

WHAT SHOULD SHE HAVE DONE?

Again, there is no finger-pointing here. The situation was as extreme as it was confusing. Later, the athlete would tell teammates that all she could think about was money for the team, for travel, and what calling out would mean to her national standing. Despite having witnesses, she would not make a formal complaint given the high stakes and competitive nature of the sport. Worse, he had previously acted as her mentor and helped her with some personal issues she had not wanted the team to know about. Now she was vulnerable in so many ways.

WHAT WOULD YOU DO?

Would you risk losing your job or standing on a team or even funding for the whole team? Would a fight be worth jeopardizing a dream of going to the Olympics? Would you be able to stand up to a wealthy aggressor threatening you with a lawsuit for defamation of character?

More importantly, do you know for a fact that you would have been able to physically fight or speak up?

With the power of your voice also comes that inner-voice – that gut-feeling you have when you know something is not right. Yet, how often do women ignore the inner-voice because we have been trained to be nice, to not offend and to be the good girl?

How often have you continued to talk to someone who gave you the creeps or walk down a hallway or street that made you uneasy, willfully ignoring all the bells and whistles going off in your head, just telling yourself you're overreacting or being ridiculous?

How many times have you allowed a relationship to continue with a person you no longer wanted any part of because you did not want to hurt that person's feelings, despite the fact that this person truly did not care about what was best for you?

You see, self-defense is so much more than punching and kicking.

11

SPEAK UP! BE HEARD! ROAR!

When was the last time you roared like a lion? No? Never?

Let's experiment:

Go to a private area – your car, a closet, the bathroom, and let 'er rip. Yell (not scream, but yell), roar and rage, as though you were warning off a dangerous predator. Yell so fiercely that even a stampeding bull would stop short and reconsider you. . . .

How did you sound? Pathetic, right? Now ask yourself, how is this sound – your power yell – going to ward off any bad guys?

By age 20, most young adults have received their high school diploma or higher. At age 16, most teenagers have earned a driver's license and most 18-year-olds are registered voters. Most adults have a bank account and, for those with a car, see to it that the oil is changed and the gas tank is full, yet how many practice a powerful, aggressive *back-off-of-me* yell?

THE DIFFERENCE BETWEEN A SCREAM AND A YELL

There is nothing wrong with a well-placed scream if it stops traffic and brings help. If, however, you need your voice to convey something else, a yell is far more effective. A yell is a warning (*back off!*), while a scream comes from fear.

YOUR GREATEST WEAPON

You probably do not have a violin case but may very well have a heavy purse. Even if you do not, however, you always have your voice. Stepping back and pointing to a roof nearby, a simple statement like, "There's a camera!" can offer enough of a distraction to save you. Whether you point out cameras or other witnesses or simply yell, the sound of your voice will tell your attacker everything, a weak-sounding voice will not ward off an aggressor. In fact, research shows that women with higher-pitched voices are not taken as seriously at work, in personal relationships, even as consumers.[1] Women with deeper or more masculine sounding voices, however, are shown to garner more respect, get more opportunities and promotions in their professional fields. Studies show that both men and women prefer the sound of masculine voices because, subjects reported, it simply sounds more authoritative. So much so that advertising agencies actively avoid using female voiceovers. Nearly 80% of all commercial voice-overs are male.[2] While we could make a strong case for sexism in the marketplace, this is a red flag in the self-defense world.

Though Chapter Eleven talks about finding your power yell, it is important to understand why the very tone of your voice is so important.

Do Not Beg

In Great Britain, schoolboy rapists reported that they believed crying was "a normal part of sex," even when this included rape and gang rape on school grounds. Unbelievably, schools were putting young rape victims back in the same classroom with their rapists. Everyday Sexism founder Laura Bates said that "the misogyny and dehumanizing nature of online pornography had made teenage boys think that making girls cry was part of foreplay."[3] In response to the escalation of schoolyard assaults, Bates created an education program to combat both the violence and ignorance.

Undeniably damaging for everyone (and more evidence for the need for more education for boys/men and girls/women), there is another disturbing pattern behind crying and/or begging victims. Assailants like it. In both heterosexual and same-sex instances, abusers feel more dominant and in control when their victim begs for help or begs not to be hurt.[4]

---

1. *https://www.ncbi.nlm.nih.gov/pubmed/19141624*

2. *https://www.bustle.com/articles/44359-the-pitch-of-your-voice-may-affect-how-successful-you-are-at-work-especially-if*

3. *https://www.thetimes.co.uk/article/boy-rapists-expect-girls-to-cry-during-sex-says-activist-7z7r06lqr*

4. *https://www.helpguide.org/articles/abuse/domestic-violence-and-abuse.htm*

My seminars repeatedly remind attendees of all ages of one fact: your attacker chose you for a reason. If the attacker is a stranger, the FBI reports that he or she may have been watching the victim anywhere from a few hours to several weeks before making a move, with ages 12 to 24 at the greatest risk and the most vulnerable to assault.[5] Therefore, begging and crying may very well be part of the assailant's game.

In the case of Abby Hernandez, she never cried. Instead, she first tried reason, telling her captor, "Look, you don't seem like a bad guy," as she promised him that if he released her immediately, he would not be in much trouble. When that did not work, she earned his trust and pretended to be a friend of sorts. Rather than being a victim, she became a co-conspirator with him.

LIVE DOWN EXPECTATIONS

As previously mentioned, the probability is high that your abuser/stalker/attacker has chosen you for a reason. A predator is an opportunist. He strikes when he believes he can without being caught which means he believes he can handle his victim through intimidation, violence, or both.

Once Abby Hernandez (Scenario 7) understood that she was trapped inside her abductor's car, her strategy was quite different. But what about those precious moments when you are still free?

Live down the predator's expectations.

The main principle of martial arts and self-defense is to walk away from a confrontation when possible, but it is imperative that you not allow yourself to be carried away, pushed down, tied up in any way. Always, ultimately, fight for your freedom and safety.

SCENARIO 13: MY BITE IS AS BIG AS MY BARK

Imagine you are taking your dog for a walk when an otherwise nice-looking man smiles at your dog and begins asking questions like, "What kind of dog he is," "How old he is," "What's his name?" and "Does he bite?" As he steps in to pet your dog, he asks, "Can I walk with you?"

---

5. *U.S. Department of Justice: National Institute of Justice. Youth Victimization: Prevalence and Implications. 2003.*

In this real-life scenario, a man approached a young girl walking the family dog in a quiet suburb. Though it was the middle of the day, the street was empty. The girl's dog was very friendly and, she knew, would offer no protection against this person. She caught a "weird feeling" about the man, politely said, "No, thank you," to his request to walk with her, and began to sidestep him. The man replied, "Oh, come on," and began to walk with her anyway.

WHAT SHOULD SHE HAVE DONE?

What the girl did not know was this same man had been identified to police as a stranger approaching two other women while walking their dogs (on separate occasions) with the same *can I walk with you* ruse. In the other two scenarios, a car or another person was present so when the women told the man "no," he left. But he made the women feel so uncomfortable, they both reported his strange behavior to the authorities. Now, a very young girl, alone on the street, was being pursued.

She should have quickly turned direction, begin running and screaming.

Remember predators select their victims for a reason and each predator typically has his or her own disguise. Serial rapists and murderer Ted Bundy liked to use a fake cast on his arm or leg and pretend to be helpless. This predator pretended to like dogs.

She should have immediately stepped back as the man approached, tightening her dog's leash so that his head was against the girl's legs and said, "Don't come too close! He bites!"

Aggressors are opportunists.

This man did not want noise. He did not want to be bitten. Presumably, he wanted to quietly walk his victim into the trees or behind a house to assault her.

She should have:

1. Pulled her dog back with the warning that "He bites!" Never allow a stranger to know if your dog is friendly or not.

2. Then, turned and run to a house where she knew someone was home, calling for help as she did so.

NOTE: In this scenario, it is important that she not run to her own home but to a dwelling that was occupied.

WHAT SHE DID DO

Awareness is Armor teaches you to put distance between yourself and your predator as quickly as possible. It is harder to grab or taser a person at a distance. However, what our girl did was a great second choice.

She used obscenities. She laid out a string of curse words and 'back off' warnings that would have made a seasoned potty-mouth blush.

It was a great strategy because her actions defied what the predator thought he knew of her. In everyday life, she was quiet, shy and never cursed but, in that moment, she decided she needed to be intimidating as well. Although he laughed at her, putting his hands up in a "whoa!" gesture, it was enough to allow her to turn and flee. We can assume that it was also enough for the man to decide that this girl was not victim material.

WHAT WOULD YOU HAVE DONE?

Be honest about what you know of yourself? Would you have felt uncomfortable but still allowed him to walk with you so as not to make a scene?

Could you let loose with a string of obscene curse words and rants of warnings? (Or would you be worried that you might be mistaken, and he might really be a nice guy?)

Would you be willing to step back, tell the person to go away, then switch directions and run?

Let's take a moment and really look at what that predator was doing.

Predators observe their victim from a distance. This means a predator can be a teacher, a coach, a neighbor or a total stranger. As the predator watches his victim, he formulates his own strategy. How will he approach? Often, then, the predator will make an initial contact or "interview" to learn more. The seemingly innocent walk with a dog would tell the predator everything he needs to know about victim, including *'Do I attack her now?'* or *'Do I come back later to her home and get her then?'*

AWARENESS

To repeat, there is no greater weapon against sexual assault than awareness. Self-awareness and situational awareness – noticing the people, cars, lighting, and activities around you is critical.

One of my students shared a story with our class that was both good and bad but served as a great example of self-awareness and self-defense. She had gone on a blind date that, she knew, was wrong from the moment she met him. He made her feel uncomfortable but because he was the friend of a friend, she ignored all the signals. Toward the end of the evening, she asked to go home, stating that she hadn't felt well. At her apartment building, however, he insisted on walking her to her door. Inside the building, he asked for her apartment key, saying he was "a gentleman" who wanted to be sure she made it inside her apartment safely.

Every sense inside her said not to hand over her key but she suppressed that feeling and complied to his request.

We've all done it. We've all allowed someone to talk to us or stand too close even though something told us it was wrong.

Why do we do that?

At her door, the moment he turned the key, everything changed. He shoved her inside and began to attack her.

We tell ourselves that "being aware of your surroundings" is only necessary when in an unfamiliar place or when you get a creepy vibe from someone. Right?

Wrong. This friend of a friend, pretending to be a *gentleman*, was extremely dangerous and she had ignored all the signs because "I was just trying to be polite and get through the evening." The good news, however, was she remembered her voice and a classic self-defense move we had practiced in class to break a handgrip.

"I yelled 'fire!' so loud the entire building lit up!"

Though she had allowed her bad guy into her building, she was also aware enough to know that her neighbors could and would hear her if she screamed bloody murder (or fire!) and her assailant ran.

WHAT IS SITUATIONAL AWARENESS?

In self-defense, situational awareness is the here and the now. It is:

- your current environment and situation
- your comprehension of your current situation
- your response to your current situation.

This is so important. Women who have never had any kind of self-defense or martial arts training tend to retract in threatening situations. Women tend to:

- look down and/or avoid eye contact with the perceived threat.

- turn their backs on the predator in an attempt to hurry away from the perceived threat.

- ignore natural instincts to call for help and use the "hope and pray" tactic to survive the situation.

THE "I ROAR; THEREFORE, I AM SAFE" TACTIC

It's time to roar.

Again, it is time to practice both your actual and your metaphorical roar.

- Pay attention to your surroundings.

- Keep your hands free. A distracted person makes for a great victim.

- Walk with confidence. Body language is everything. Chin up, back straight, eyes always scanning the crown, project an air of confidence.

What better time than to introduce Leigh Ann?

SCENARIO 14: THE STORY OF LEIGH ANN

Leigh Ann Floyd was doing everything right. She attended kickboxing classes twice a week, had taken self-defense classes, and was physically strong. But, like all of us, she had a moment of bad judgment. She was in the historic downtown Fort Worth stockyards in Texas where she met up with some friends for a couple of hours. When she decided it was time to head back to her car, she took a short-cut through an alley. Then she realized that she had company behind her and quickened her pace but, it seemed, so did the man behind her. Panic flooded her thoughts.

As she tells the story, she thought about what she had learned in our kickbox and self-defense classes.

Your voice is your greatest weapon.

Use your voice.

Surprise your aggressor.

Have the upper hand.

Your voice is your greatest weapon.

She turned on him like a rabid dog, charging and barking. Yes. Barking.

The man halted, hands up. "Whoa!"

Then Leigh Ann turned and ran for her car. As she struggled, hands trembling, to get her car door open, the man emerged from the alley. He was coming toward her! At last, she was able to turn the lock and get into her car, watching the approaching man in her rearview mirror as she fumbled to get the key into the ignition. She readied herself for what was to come. Then, she said, "He got into the car behind me."

As she recounted this story to a kickboxing class, her classmates howled with laughter and Leigh Ann, a sheepish grin on her face, could only shake her head. "I was so embarrassed."

WHAT WOULD YOU DO?

Be honest. Most women would have simply prayed that they were just being paranoid and hoped to make it out of the alley alive. A smaller population would have broken into a run. About 2% would have done as Leigh Ann did.

Genuinely ask yourself what you would have done. Would you have been able to turn, charge and bark?

What would you have done?

The bigger question is why would so few have done as Leigh Ann did? Why aren't women willing to protect themselves? Why do so many "hope and pray" to make it out alive when all they have to do is turn, charge and bark?

It is such an easy thing to do. Turn. Charge. Bark.

But Leigh Ann was wrong. The guy was just a guy – not a predator. (She thinks.) While her fellow classmates laughed at the story, they also applauded her.

Leigh Ann did the right thing.

That was awesome.

I'll bet that guy will think twice before following a woman so closely in a darkened alleyway.

Now you've got a great story to tell!

But there was something much more important about Leigh Ann's proactive charging and barking. While the above comments are all true, one thing was immediately made clear to her classmates:

Leigh Ann found her power. Leigh Ann found her power yell. Her willingness to protect herself and her creativity in shocking her presumed aggressor did more than potentially save her; Leigh Ann discovered herself. When asked the important question: "Would you be able to do that again?" Leigh Ann was adamant. *Yes!*

Women and girls are so conditioned by cultural norms to be kind, patient, sweet, and forgiving that it is to our own detriment.

Consider this: In polygamist societies here in the United States, survivors report that they are told from early childhood that girls are to remain "sweet" at all times. By demanding the "be sweet" code of conduct, the boys and men who abuse them are guaranteed control over the behavior of these girls and women. "Be sweet" demands that the girls and women comply with the polygamists' horrific abuse.

In May 2017, the United Nations conducted a survey in just four Middle Eastern countries (Egypt, Morocco, Lebanon and Palestine) where the vast majority of men admitted to sexually harassing women in public, ranging from ogling and derogatory comments to sexual groping and rape because it was "fun." Of those men, 90% agreed that women who dressed provocatively deserved to be heckled and/or assaulted and that women like being sexually harassed as it is "positive attention."[6]

As long as the world stays mute on the issues of domestic abuse and honor killings (the killing of a female relative who is perceived to have brought dishonor on the family), sexual harassment and the degradation of females simply because they are females, these behaviors will persist worldwide. Our sisters in nations in the Middle East, Africa, and elsewhere that ignore the abuse of women are still *our sisters*. Their torment is our torment. And just because a woman is a victim of sexual assault in a nation that accepts such barbaric behaviors as the norm doesn't make it any less criminal or horrific.

---

6. *Cauterucci, Christina, "Do Women Like Being Sexually Harassed? Men in New Survey Say Yes." Slate Magazine. June 19, 2017*

WHERE ARE THE HEROES?

When we see news stories about women who were harassed and/or assaulted with witnesses (other men) who did nothing at the time, one must wonder why they did nothing. Perhaps, like many victims, these men did not want to believe what they were seeing. Later, however, when they were asked to testify or speak up but refused, we have to wonder how they can live with themselves.

How can they hold their heads up?

How can they pretend to love their own mothers, daughters or sisters, wives or girlfriends yet allow this to happen to someone else's?

If we are to believe Hollywood, these men were supposed to be the heroes. They were supposed to save the female victim. So, why didn't they?

In a study on men and masculinities, researcher and professor Michael Kimmel found that the hero mentality is still alive – for men. It's for the protection of men and masculinity. Kimmel explains why men are slow to speak up in protection of a woman when they see her being harassed or assaulted. "We're afraid that if we do, we'll be marginalized, kicked out of the men's club … Men know that doing the right thing sometimes carries costs, and most of us are worried about jeopardizing what we have. So, we betray the women in the room, abandon our ethics, and slink away uncomfortably."[7]

The research revealed what we've always known: the hierarchy among males is too valuable for other males, even witnesses to a crime, to upset. By questioning another man on his behavior toward a woman, he is marginalizing the male status of the predator. It is then, according to this code, better to allow the female to be marginalized.

Although this information is upsetting, it is not surprising; it is yet another example of why you must be your own hero.

Know that even as these words go to print, there are those upset that the behavior of men has been questioned (thus marginalized) despite the fact that countless female victims have fallen prey to well-known, wealthy predators while male business partners, friends and/or associates did and said nothing because it would mess with the 'bro

---

7. *https://hbr.org/2018/01/getting-men-to-speak-up*

code.' While times are changing, we should not rely on others to save us. Thus, the story of Leigh Ann.

THE LESSONS OF LEIGH ANN

Watching Leigh Ann retell the story of her alleged attacker is fun. As she reenacts that moment when she realized her would-be "rapist" just wanted to get into his own car, she slumps with humiliation and every woman listening laughs with empathy.

But her embarrassment is also critical because it points to one of main reasons (if not the main reason) why women do not yell and scream when threatened. *What if we're wrong?*

This is an important point to remember: Any man worth his salt is not going to be angry with a woman for defending herself against a potential assault. Any decent man would understand why a woman would have been frightened in that scenario and could not possibly be angry with her for defending herself. Leigh Ann not only learned something about herself, but she taught that man a valuable lesson about following women into darkened alleys.

What she learned about herself is that she is amazing. She is brave. She used her voice and protected her number one – Leigh Ann. And even as we teased that somewhere there is a man now terrified to walk down darkened alleys if a woman is nearby, we all rolled with laughter because we were so proud of her. *Ya did good, Leigh Ann. Ya did good.*

In nations where women are daily subjected to violence and degradation in accordance to cultural norms, it is unfair to ask that they raise their voices – though we can hope. For women in Western and, supposedly, more advanced nations where women's rights are concerned, it is always unfair to judge how one woman responds to her own personal assault. As a people, however, as a collective group, we can help each other find our voices. But it starts today with just one – yours.

DON'T JUST SPEAK UP – ROAR!

This is it: You're being attacked. It is not just about yelling. It is about making your assailant rethink the idea that you are an easy target.

Remember this: The act of aggression is NOT about you. It has nothing to do with your beauty or charm. This is a power trip for some sicko through violence and degradation. You need to speak to your assailant in a manner he can understand. This assault, this crime is about him and his own power trip, so he needs to be reminded of what *he* has to lose. If you are in a public setting, remind him:

- "I just called 911."

- "You don't want to do this. There are multiple witnesses."

- "Ever heard of technology? There are literally seven cameras surrounding us. Every angle of this assault is being recorded."

Particularly when the assailant knows his victim (and vice versa), there is often too much to lose in this scenario. Be prepared for the fact that he will call you "bitch," "tease," "instigator," and claim you misled him, but the idea is to make him think about long-term repercussions for *him*.

If he is a stranger, be emotionally prepared for him to call you names and say degrading and threatening things designed to shut you up and shut you down.

In a setting that is still public but where the assailant is a stranger, the advantage is still yours as you are in public and can use modern technology (aka – evidence) in your favor. If, however, you are in a remote, more secluded area and not even your power yell can illicit outside help, your demeanor can still command attention. Rather than beg or cry, which does not work, bellow vulgar, loud threats, bad language, and the promise of horrible things AS you are getting ready for the fight of your life.

Be the exact opposite of what your assailant wanted.

Defend you.

Fight for you.

Go practice your roar.

12

OH, THE GAMES WE PLAY
Learning to Identify Your "Bad Guy"

In my self-defense seminars, there are four major points to the lecture:

1. Listen to and respect your inner voice.

2. Roar – your power yell.

3. Walk Tall and Play the "I See You" Game

4. Game on!

Make no mistake: The roar (both literal and figurative) is important. But because aggressors are opportunistic, they do not choose victims they believe will roar mightily in public any more than they choose a victim they think will fight back.

They look for someone who looks uncertain, is afraid to fight back, afraid to speak up, or is unable (or unwilling) to roar. In the corporate, sports, academic, literary, healthcare, entertainment, restaurant and hospitality worlds, to name but a few, aggressors will also look for someone who is afraid to speak out for fear of losing a job, a promotion, a title, a position, a grade, or a review. They look for victims who can be silenced through intimidation.

There is no greater example of this than a former beauty pageant owner. From 1996 to 2015, he owned the Miss Universe Organization, including Miss USA and Miss Teen USA, until he was forced to sell the organization in 2015. During that time, there were multiple complaints about him walking into the dressing rooms of beauty queens as they changed clothing, including many repeated walk-ins on Miss Teen contestants. In 2005, the owner appeared on the *Howard Stern Show* and bragged that he would walk in while teenage girls were getting dressed, saying, "You know, no men are anywhere. And I'm allowed to go in because I'm the owner of the pageant. And therefore, I'm inspecting it... 'Is everyone okay?' You know, they're standing there with no clothes. 'Is everyone okay?' And you see these incredible-looking women, and so, I sort of get away with things like that."[1] And this same man publicly admitted that he was more sexually attracted to his own daughter than his wife.

This man embodied the FBI's profile of a sexual predator and yet he was a well-known and successful businessman, so his actions were ignored and/or excused.

The complaints about inappropriate hugging, kissing on the lips, public degrading, and frequent appearances backstage while contestants were naked or half-naked were plentiful, but there appeared to be no stopping this man. As the owner, in bragging about his lascivious behaviors, he was emboldened by his own power. He knew that the girls and women might complain to one another but would never go public with any complaints as it would only get them kicked out of his beauty pageant.

This is how predators operate. And when we do not speak up, those who attack will attack again. And again. And again. And with each assault and the continued degradation of our fellow sisters, such monsters grow in confidence, insulting female leaders, entrepreneurs, educators and pioneers for being strong, independent, and smart – all things that aggressors do not like in a female.

WALK TALL AND MAKE EYE CONTACT

The expression "walk tall" means to walk with an air of confidence and self-assurance, to have pride in oneself and pride in one's own actions.

This is it.

There is no magic equation here. Walking tall is easy. Take everything you have read and apply it to your walk. Here goes:

- Be aware of your surroundings.

- Stay off the cell phone while in public.

- Make mental notes of who you pass, how they approach you, and keep a respectful distance from those you do not know or who might give off a bad vibe.

---

1. Stuart, Tessa, "A Timeline of Donald Trump's Creepiness While He Owned Miss Universe." Rolling Stone Magazine. October 12, 2016

- Make eye contact.

- Walk tall – head up, face the world, shoulders squared, exuding confidence.

Easier said than done?

No. Even for the most timid and/or insecure person, practice can make for a taller walk! Just as you need to practice your yell, you can practice how you walk and how you are perceived.

This is the third component of the lesson – walking tall and learning to look at people. In having self- and situational awareness, you begin to truly pay attention to what and who is around you. Let's go.

PRACTICE CONFIDENCE

- Start with a "hello." As you pass people, say, "hi." For shy people, this is a difficult task, but it is empowering. As you do this more and more, you will notice how many people do not make eye contact. You're in control with the "hello." But it also ensures that you know what people look like. You are aware. You are personally and situationally aware!

- Strong spine. Did you know that when you drop your head to read your text messages (the average adult head weighs between 10 to 12 pounds), upwards of 60 pounds of pressure pulls on your spine? With the average American sending/receiving 128 texts per day, imagine how much this changes the individual spine and how we stand. Pinch your shoulders back, lift your chin, and just watch how differently people look at you. You are walking tall.

- Adopt a mantra. Whether you tell yourself you are brave or strong, you are loved or needed, remind yourself of your worth. You are entitled to respect, courtesy and safety.

CONTINUE TO GROW YOUR CONFIDENCE

- Stay Self-Aware: Always know where you are going, who you will be with and who may be watching you.

- Recognize your weaknesses and create an on-going list of how you might improve them. For example, if you are weak in strength, find the resolve to get in better shape. Learn to box. Learn to fight. Make new friends in doing this. If you are shy, joining a fitness class just might break you out of your comfort zone. If you are unable to do these things due to physical limitations, empower yourself in different ways: join a book club and suggest reading books on empowerment; attend lectures on self-defense on a regular basis, etc.

• When out in public, have a call button you can always press or an open line on the phone and tell your phone friend, "Yup, I'm passing a guy who looks like .." "Oh, and now I'm on 73rd Street and …," but be sure you are not distracted by chitchat. Have these "safety calls" be all about your own personal safety.

• Recognize your strengths and capitalize on them. Make your presence and persona strong. If you are in a wheelchair or use a walker, your presence is still strong with a strong voice, a steely gaze, and an open phone line!

• Believe in yourself. Practice your own private mantra until you believe what you are saying. You are your own #1.

• Do not be afraid of being hurt. If you are chosen to be a victim, you may very likely be hurt. Be prepared to fight for yourself. Repeat: You are your own #1.

• Know that it is okay to be scared or feel threatened, but you must still stand up for yourself. You must still roar.

THE ART OF EYE CONTACT (MAKE A GAME OF IT!)

In developing your confidence as you walk, you are also developing new situational awareness skills that could save your life. For many, however, making eye contact is so intimidating that most do not do it and, despite knowing better, continue to walk with eyes downcast.

So, play a game:

Identify features. Every day, identify a different feature (physical or one of attitude) in people and count how many you see each time you are on public streets, taking public transportation, or jogging along a quiet path. Count how many times you see someone with a mustache, wearing mirrored sunglasses, walking with an altered gait (a limp, a stoop, etc), or wearing boots. In doing so, you are always scanning the horizon. Fixate on a number.

As you jog, you want to see five dogs, seven people wearing earbuds, and five people wearing hats. On the metro, you want to see nine people wearing Reeboks, four people reading books, 10 people talking on their phones, and seven people wearing gold chains.

Actively make yourself look for different characteristics and/or physical descriptions. In doing so, you *will* make eye contact with people, you will be aware of the movement of people and, most importantly, you will appear more confident, alert and less suitable to be a victim.

Developing your confidence means developing your self-worth and self-esteem. It means learning to walk tall, speak up, and listen to that inner-voice telling you that something (or someone) is wrong. It means redefining the word "victim" because it is not or will no longer be you.

13

THE MURDER OF
MISSY BEVERS

As of this printing, Missy's murder remains unsolved and, it is believed, the murderer is still at large in Missy's hometown. On April 18, 2016, Missy, a fitness instructor, arrived early on a rainy Monday morning to a church in Midlothian, Texas, that had agreed to let her teach class indoors during inclement weather. She had even posted on her Facebook account, "If it's raining, we're still training," giving the time and place for class. When she arrived, well before the scheduled 5 a.m. class time to set up her training equipment, Missy was ambushed and brutally murdered.

Though the details are horrific, her story bears telling for three very important reasons:

1. Because her murder is still unsolved (despite actual videos on YouTube in which the murderer can be seen strolling throughout the church wearing tactical SWAT gear, waiting for Missy to arrive to kill her), it needs to be told again and again until her murderer is caught.

2. In the days, months, then years that followed, many began to conclude that some of the victim's own behavior may have led to her brutal death. This is intolerable. Missy did not deserve this. No one deserves this. This needs to be discussed.

3. Missy actually participated in a one-time, very short self defenseclass which, at its conclusion, Missy recognized she needed to do more.

THE UNSOLVED MURDER CASE OF MISSY BEVERS

Missy entered the building, in the pre-dawn hours, alone, arms full of gear and equipment, only to be ambushed. Her assailant was wearing tactical police gear, was armed with multiple weapons, and had physical size, strength, and the element of surprise on his side.

The word '*his*' in regard to the assailant remains a topic of debate.

It is not the purpose of this book or my self defense classes to speculate beyond what is absolutely known. Media outlets reported stories of a strained marriage, financial problems, odd behaviors from Bevers' husband and in-laws, and video footage that compares the killer's walk to possible suspects, but the purpose here is to analyze (without judgement) what we do know.

WHAT SHOULD SHE HAVE DONE?

One could argue that Missy broke many safety rules. She was alone. She used social media to tell everyone where she would be at a specific time and place – a time and place in which there would be, ever so briefly, no witnesses. She was distracted. And she also had been previously threatened.

The reality, however, is that this was her job. Early morning fitness instructors everywhere have empathized with this scenario but ultimately understand it is part of the job. Unfortunately, this is where we all become complacent.

For that matter, all around the world there are professions in which a man or woman must open a business or walk down empty streets well before sunrise to get to or to do their job. In the case of Missy, however, not only was this early morning set-up mandatory for her job so, too, was posting online. Because Camp Gladiator constantly moves locations, it was essential to her business that she let her people know where they could find her.

Readers do not need to be told what she should have done. We all know. And therein lies the rub. We've all done it. We've all taken that risk of knowing that parking in an underground parking garage late at night or walking a back alley or entering an empty, darkened building could hold great danger but we … *shrug it off*.

Missy's horrific murder reminds us all of what we instinctually know.

WHAT WOULD YOU HAVE DONE?

Be honest. Would you have asked a friend or relative to get up with you at 4 a.m. to drive across town in the pouring rain to set up weights and gear for a class that they could then participate in but would not be paid for?

When this very question was posed to more than 100 fitness instructors, 100% of the answers came in the way of a laugh, followed by some variation of a "no way."[1]

Although Missy should have had someone with her, she was presumably too nice to ask anyone for help. And, let's be honest. Had Missy asked a friend to be with her that fateful morning, who knows what the outcome would have been? If you do find the videos on line of Missy's killer walking the halls of the church prior to the murder, you'll find a vengeful, dangerous predator patiently awaiting his targeted prey. In this terrible instance, might he have also killed the friend?

Mercifully, in that scenario, we will never know.

But there is something else to consider here: the threatening message.

Less than three days before her murder, Missy received a "creepy" message online. Reportedly, she showed this message "from a male unknown" to a friend. Both had agreed that the message "was creepy and strange."[2]

Had only this message been saved and documented, perhaps police could have found who threatened her, but Missy deleted it, and her friend could not remember further details.

Would you have saved and documented a "creepy" message?

What if you thought it a joke? Would you shrug it off and delete it or still document it and report it? Had she contacted the police, might this have then prompted someone to tell her not to be alone during early morning set-ups for class? Would you really insist that someone travel with you to a possibly unsafe area and/or document questionable messages directed at you?

THE MISCONCEPTION OF MISSY... AND HER MUSCLES

Much was made about Missy's fitness in regard to her murder that are false, misleading, and unfair.

---

1. *DallasMANIA*

2. *https://www.cbsnews.com/news/docs-church-murder-victim-terri-missy-bevers-received-creepy-linkedin-message/*

Almost as soon as it was discovered who the victim was, the speculation began. *The murderer had to be someone strong because Missy was so strong* and *the killer had police training of some kind, otherwise no way would Missy go down.* Again and again, pictures of Missy's impressive biceps were highlighted as evidence that she could have only been taken down by someone well-trained and powerful.

In reality, she never had a chance. Her murderer – a coward who hid in the dark, hidden behind a costume and armed to the teeth — blindsided her. It doesn't matter if Missy had been the Incredible Hulk or the very petite woman that she was, the actions of this particular coward could have taken just about anyone down. The greatest of fighters, men and women dedicated to mixed martial arts, military tactical warfare, and police training, have been brought down by a single shot. In the case of Missy, while details to the public have been sparse, police believe Missy had no real chance of surviving such an assault.

It is important to remember that just because someone has the appearance of a strong body does not mean he or she can fight. Conversely, just because someone looks like a wimp doesn't mean they may not be dangerous. In the world of self-defense, appearance means very little. How you carry yourself, however, is something different.

We'll never know if Missy recognized her attacker or, perhaps, thought him a police officer and therefore did not initially flee. We can only take lessons from a woman who was dedicated to helping others. She was so focused on setting up her exercise equipment, she was an easy target.

Do not allow yourself to be in a situation where there is no help to be found in an emergency. Do not run or hike in areas so remote that you are an easy target. If your work or travel plans require you to be in an isolated area, bring a friend. It is perfectly reasonable to ask a police or security officer, or someone from your company or school to meet you at the location. Do not be afraid to ask.

Never dismiss a threatening message or phone call. A threat is a threat. Take it seriously.

Do not delude yourself into thinking that completing one self-defense class will protect you. Self-defense is a life-long process in learning self- and situational awareness, and how to act and react to those around you. *And always remember that there is no greater possession than self-worth.*

14

MORE THAN JUST LOCKER ROOM TALK

Our entire lives we've heard those expressions of "Boys will be boys" and "It's just locker room talk." However, if we are to truly understand and appreciate what self-defense is, we must also understand how harmful words are because the acceptance of certain words leads to how we later interpret actions.

Insulting, demeaning, and violent talk about attacking women can lead to aggressive behavior against women. It certainly does not mean that all boys or men who engage in this kind of talk will be aggressive, but some will. And have.

In locker rooms across the nation, there is a rise in violent and degrading attitudes about girls/women in high school, collegiate and professional locker rooms. Particularly with college and professional athletes, victims are publicly disgraced, even threatened, to drop any charges against athletes as play time equals money. Humanity be damned.

Studies have shown that while male student athletes make up only 3% of the student population, they perpetrate 19% of sexual assaults and 35% of domestic assaults, with 54% of college athletes admitting to "perpetrating some form of sexual coercion." Worst of all, one in three college rapes is committed by an athlete.[1]

A study by North Carolina State University, the University of South Florida, Northern Arizona University and Emory University found that male college athletes are more likely than college students in general (non-athletes) "to commit sexual violence or engage in sexual coercion." Athletes were also more likely to believe in rape myths "such as that if a woman is drunk or doesn't fight back, it isn't rape" and to harbor more traditional, and frequently negative, beliefs about women, such as that

---

1. *http://www.northeastern.edu/rugglesmedia/2016/10/28/sports-and-cultures-of-violence-a-look-back-at-major-incidents*

"Women should worry less about their rights and more about becoming good wives and mothers." These beliefs, the researchers found, were a factor in the athletes' higher rate of sexual assault.[2]

An ESPN "Outside the Lines" special found that college athletes are three times more likely than other students to be accused of sexual misconduct or domestic violence at Power 5 conference schools, although the schools seem to be less than enthusiastic about investigating those charges. Half of Title IX complaints involve athletes.

"The [special] also cited a 2017 study — published in a journal called *Violence Against Women* — that covered sexual coercion practices among undergraduate athletes showing that they were '77% more likely to engage in sexual coercion than non-athletes,' and that athletes reported less positive attitudes toward women and greater acceptance of rape myths, with one example being that "women make false allegations of sexual assault to target innocent men.'"[3]

This dangerous and pervasive mentality among college athletes will not let up as long as our culture idolizes athletes and gives them a pass on their bad behavior, starting with the schools. Historically speaking, universities and colleges provide support to the student athlete accused of rape while completely neglecting the victim. Universities have been known to provide strippers for athlete recruits and use attractive female students as "hosts" for recruits. No wonder these young men don't take women seriously.

Not surprisingly, the behavior doesn't stop after college. A study done by a University of Texas at Dallas Criminologist to refute the notion of criminal athletes found that NFL players are actually arrested about half as much as the general population. "There's a perception that the NFL has this huge crime problem and that it's longstanding. That's what everybody believes," said one of the study's authors, Dr. Alex Piquero. What was NOT emphasized in the study, however, was that the exceptions were violent crime. NFL players, in fact, had a higher arrest rate for violent crimes. Domestic abuse was not factored into the statistics because the NFL and FBI do not collect that data.[4]

---

2. *https://www.sciencedaily.com/releases/2016/06/160602095206.htm*

3. *https://www.espn.com/espn/otl/story/_/id/25149259/college-athletes-three-s-more-likely-named-title-ix-sexual-misconduct-complaints*

4. *https://www.utdallas.edu/news/reasearch/ut-dallas-criminologist-tackles-perception-of-nfl/#:~:text=News%20Center%20%C2%BB%20Research-,UT%20Dallas%20Criminologist%20Tackles%20Perception%20of%20NFL%20Players,Crime%20Rate%20Than%20General%20Population*

Interestingly, even as this book was being written, this author was contacted by a major state university that had experienced a rash of assaults on young women on its campus. The university wanted to keep the outbreak of violence quiet as *the image* of college students being assaulted on the university's own campus, dispelling the idea of a safe environment, was bad for business. It did, however, want to educate the female population. But the problem was and is not with the female students. The problem is with the predators and those who condone that way of thinking. As long as people accept the 'boys will be boys' mentality, we have a problem.

LOCKER ROOM – BOARD ROOM – CLASSROOM TALK

If we accept that males are allowed to disrespect, disparage, and dishonor females as long as it is funny (to the males), the problem persists. For those who find humor in the insults and sexual references or who share a chuckle with teammates or co-workers, they argue the demeaning remarks are harmless and the rest of us need to get over it.

Even for the men who know better and don't especially like locker room talk, studies show that the majority of males go along with it for fear of being considered less manly by peers.[5]

As long as we ignore this kind of behavior, the silence is acceptance to those perpetuating the belief that women are not of equal standing and/or importance to men. When someone (or even something) is continuously diminished overtime, she or he (or it) loses value.

HOW DO WE STOP THIS?

Believe it or not, we can stop the locker room treatment of girls and women. Here's how:

- You know how people like to joke that someone "fights like a girl," or "acts like a girl" but it's meant as an insult? Call them on it! *You mean, fights like Ronda Rousey, who could easily beat up any man in America?*

- Do not allow for a female assault victim to be judged because of what she was wearing or if she was drunk. No girl or woman asks

---

5. Paresky, Pamela B., Phd, "What's Wrong with Locker Room Talk? Boys will be Boys," *Psychology Today*. October 10, 2016.

to be assaulted. Do not let anyone insinuate a victim deserved rape.

• Do not tolerate anyone to say a woman should just "get over" being sexually harassed at work because the man was *kidding* or *just trying to be nice*! No man would ever ignore being harassed and made to feel horrible at work each day.

• Beware of trigger words against females: girls are "just" a girl, over-reactive, emotional, dramatic, etc.

• Don't judge the victim. When a victim finds the courage to name her (or his) assault, never ask "Why did you wait so long to speak out?"

• Argue that males and females can "just be friends. For those who say guys can't be friends with the opposite sex, ask why? Clearly, there are much bigger issues about respect if a male can only think of a female in sexual (dating) terms.

Besides the good 'ol boy banter about girls and women, there is also the girl talk and it's a doozy. Just as dangerous as the "just a girl" and "just locker room talk" mentality is the "You know how women are" mentality:

• You know how it is when you get a group of women together.

• Women are just mean.

The more we keep saying that, the truer it becomes. Even with evidence to prove otherwise. Research from the University of Zurich revealed that women's brains (biology) make females kinder, gentler, more tolerant and accepting.[6] So why do we all continue to bad-mouth women?

We must be more proactive in how women are portrayed, treated, and respected in our own communities. Here's your checklist on how to help:

• Stop repeating expressions that are demeaning to women, such as, "You know how women are." *You* are a female. Stop demeaning yourself! If your friend is being a jerk, she's being a jerk, and this has nothing to do with being a female.

---

6. Petter, Olivia. "Women are Kinder and More Generous Than Men, Study Finds," Independent. October 10, 2017.

- Recognize that men engage in indirect aggressive behaviors like gossiping and social exclusion just as frequently as women. In fact, studies have shown that men can be worse.[7]

- Stop negative female speak when you hear it.

- Recognize that media images promote a woman's worth through being slender, sexy, and vulnerable. Stop allowing and/or endorsing this depiction. Refuse music, movies, TV shows, and books where women are perpetual victims without a voice and without justice.

- Beware of the girl who brags "All my friends are guys," thinking it somehow makes her better. Sadly, she's thrown her own kind under the bus for the wrong kind of popularity. Do not buy into her claims that "Girls are too mean." This is factually incorrect.

Know this: We are a powerful voting bloc. Women are the world's leading consumers and, in the next decade, are slated to be the beneficiaries of the largest transference of wealth in U.S. history. Women have exceeded men in earning both undergraduate and graduate degrees in college and are the majority of the U.S. workforce. We hold the majority of managerial positions and, now entering the political arena, are changing laws and decision-making processes faster than ever before.

In short, we freaking rock.

But what does this all have to do with self-defense, self-awareness, your attacker, and changing how we view (and treat) women?

Everything. Absolutely everything.

When we accept and acknowledge that we are powerful leaders and innovators; that we are changing the political landscape; and influencing business, marketing and laws, we can stop accepting the negative talk (and abuse) against women.

We deserve much better.

---

7. Forrest, S., V. Eatough, M. Shevlin, "Measuring Adult Indirect Aggression: The Development and Psychometric Assessment of the Indirect Aggression Scales." Aggressive Behavior. Vol. 31, pages 84-97, 2005.

15

FIGHT, FLIGHT OR... FREEZE?

Beloved *Charmed* actress Rose McGowan froze.

It was not a scene from the popular TV show but in real life when she was rendered helpless both physically and cognitively as her assailant raped her.

Historically speaking, few women in Hollywood had ever been brave enough to speak out against powerful directors but, bit by bit, McGowan began to speak up. And she wasn't alone. As the #MeToo movement gathered steam, thousands of women came forward to publicly share their stories of assault and many disclosed stories of *freezing*. As actress Kristina Cohen describes an assault by a famous TV actor, her words are all too familiar to other victims: "I was paralyzed, terrified. I couldn't speak, I could no longer move."[1]

The issue of freezing is real.

This is yet another reason why victim-blaming is not only intolerable but biologically incorrect: For decades, self-defense taught the "fight or flight" methods, never giving any consideration to the idea of freezing? To freeze was, in the minds of most, pathetic. It was a total give up and, in the fight world, unforgivable.

New evidence, however, reveals that not only is the freeze instinct real, it is biological. A 2017 study in Stockholm pokes gaping holes in the archaic arguments that if the victim did not fight back, it was not rape. Yet, as recently as late 2016, a judge in Italy ruled in favor of a rapist because his victim did not scream or fight enough to call the attack rape. The victim, who was abused as a child by her father, freezes "with

---

1. *https://www.nydailynews.com/entertainment/hollywood-stars-accused-sexual-harassment-assault-gallery-1.3547625*

people who are too strong." To add more injury to the victim, she now faces slander charges lodged against her by her assailant.[2]

The Swedish study, published in the journal *Acta Obstetricia et Gynecologica Scandinavica*, found that tonic immobility, believed to be an evolutionary defense mechanism in animals (look up fainting goats), also exists in humans. Tonic immobility causes the body to freeze when the animal or human is unable to fight back. The results of this particular study showed that it was normal for rape victims to experience temporary paralysis, thus rendering them unable to strongly resist or call for help. The study, including almost 300 women who went to an emergency room in Stockholm following assaults, found that 70% of the victims experienced tonic immobility during the attack. Of those, 50% reported extreme, almost catatonic, paralysis.[3]

How many times have we heard or read about an attack in which the victim reportedly froze, went mute, or described her attack as an out-of-body experience in which she could not move? Yet she would be blamed for not fighting back.

As it happens, the entire "fight or flight" discussion in self-defense, law enforcement, and rape crisis centers around the world, is hotly debated.

Here are some facts you need to consider:

• Some domestic violence and rape crisis centers teach that fighting the attacker may cause more harm or even death to the victim. This is misleading. It is true that fighting back could cause more harm because a fight does mean you can be hurt. However, what does it mean if you do not fight? Do you really think you won't be harmed in a rape?

• One U.S. study examined 1.5 million assault victims over the course of a decade and determined that women who fought back were more likely to get away, but the fight did increase incidents of injury by 10%.

• Every scenario, every assault, every victim and every predator are different. Because of this, it is essential that women take self-de-

---

2. Phillips, Kristine. "A Sexual Assault Case was Tossed Because the Woman Didn't Scream During Alleged Attack," Washington Post. March 26, 2017.

3. Pearson, Catherine. "Why So Many Rape Victims Don't Simply 'Fight Back'," HuffPost. August 4, 2017.

fense courses to prepare and better enable themselves to read and react to different situations.

- Not fighting off an attacker leads to greater levels of anxiety, remorse, stress, and guilt. In a study of women who did and did not fight their rapists but were all victims of rape, those who did not fight experienced greater episodes of post-traumatic stress syndrome, recurring nightmares and re-living the attacks, guilt and anxiety.

- It's not just female victims. In fact, it is very common for male victims, no matter the age, to freeze as well. (See Chapter 16: Male Survivors of Sexual Assault.)

In the Swedish study, researchers discovered that the victims who experienced tonic immobility or temporary paralysis were at higher risk of PTSD and depression following the rape. And though they could not help their own reaction and immobility to the attack, they then blamed themselves for not fighting back. The long-term emotional damage from this is immeasurable.

The reality is we can talk about what we should do in the event of a predatory attack all day long. Until you are face-to-face with an assailant, you do not know how you will react. It is why the story of Leigh Ann is so wonderful as she turned on her imagined attacker, chasing and barking like a dog to scare him off. It does not matter that she may have been wrong about the man's intentions; she discovered that she would be able to react in her time of need. She has great comfort in this. For women who did not or were physically/emotionally unable to fight back, an unspeakably horrible assault is then compounded by one's own guilt and remorse. This heartbreaking truth is further evidence of why we must educate all people about the realities of rape and the rape culture. That an innocent person could be so tortured by the criminal act of another person and, worse, one who most typically goes free is unacceptable. According to RAINN, a national anti-sexual violence organization, "Perpetrators of sexual violence are less likely to go to jail or prison than other criminals."[4] Just another reason to be as proactive as you can in your own welfare.

So how can you un-freeze yourself in a crisis?

---

4. *https://www.rainn.org/statistics/criminal-justice-system*

A study published in the *Journal of Interpersonal Violence* demonstrated the importance of self-defense training, using data from 3,187 female college students. Women with what the researchers termed pre-assault training were more likely to head off an attack (remember self-awareness and situational awareness) but were also less scared and ready to defend themselves before the assault than those women without any training.[5]

With continued self-defense training and/or sexual assault prevention education comes opportunities to discuss different scenarios, role-play, and better prepare for the what-ifs. These scenarios allow women to become more assertive, confident, and in control – all very empowering tools every woman and man should possess.

Trending slogans and hashtags like #TimesUp! are wonderful but are just words unless we make it real. This is your time to empower and embolden **you**!

---

5. *Brecklin, L, Ullman, S.E., "Self-Defense or Assertiveness Training and Women's Responses to Sexual Attacks." Journal of Interpersonal Violence. 2005 June; Vol. 20 (6): pages 738-62.*

16

MALE SURVIVORS OF SEXUAL ASSAULT

In *Chapter Eleven: Speak Up! Be Heard! Roar!*, we discussed how men are fearful of speaking out against other men in defense of a female for fear of "being kicked out of the men's club." In a section that is entitled, "Where Are the Heroes?" the importance of male status in society is analyzed with the purposeful use of the word "hero." Despite the fact that the majority of breadwinners in the United States are women, despite the fact that the majority of people with higher education are women, despite the fact that women are climbing the corporate level at record pace, the majority of men still view women as lesser status. Men are most always the heroes in movies just as the more *heroic* professions and sports are overwhelmingly male dominated. Men also still view sexual crime as a female problem.

Imagine, then, being a victim of sexual assault as a boy or man.

As historically difficult as this issue has been for females to discuss, how incapacitating must this be for a male?

According to numerous studies, including the U.S. Centers for Disease Control and Prevention, one in every six boys in sexually abused before their 18th birthday. One in four men experience "unwanted sexual events" during their lifetime.[1] These numbers exclude rape victims within the prison system (an important distinction but certainly not to be undermined). Yet, shocking as the numbers are, they are probably low because males are much less likely to disclose them – or even consider themselves to have been sexually abused.

In 2013, however, the National Crime Victimization Survey revealed that 38% of sexual assaults were against men. Just as the Harvey Weinstein outrage brought forth the #MeToo movement in a great wave, the Jerry

---

1. *https://www.psychiatrictimes.com/view/other-me-too-male-sexual-abuse-survivors*

Sandusky and Penn State sex scandal in 2011 and the subsequent media coverage should have empowered more male victims to come forward. It did not.

While the #MeToo movement has empowered many, too many male victims remain silent for fear of being marginalized.

How bad is it? When language in surveys about molestation was changed to include the molestation and/or coercion of boys, including unwanted oral sex and anal sex and "'being made to penetrate'" someone else with their own body parts, either by physical force or coercion, or when the victim was drunk or high or otherwise unable to consent, the statistics jumped from one in every 71 men to one in every six – a staggering difference and more evidence in how the "macho" culture adversely affects us all.[2]

And just like their female counterparts, these victims suffer from severe depression, anxiety, fear of public scrutiny and shame. Perhaps because male victims are far less likely to report the crime, they also have higher instances of alcoholism, drug abuse, suicidal thoughts and attempts, and PTSD.[3] Not only are men more like to abuse drugs and/or alcohol to cope, they are more likely to respond with anger and later become abusers themselves.

For male victims, their own response to an assault can be more biologically confusing than that of a female. Some boys or men may actually get an erection during the assault that is both confusing to the victim and empowering to the predator. While the victim has guilt and embarrassment by this physiological reaction (*Why did that happen? Did I enjoy it deep-down but just can't admit it? Is something wrong with me? Did I ask for that to happen?*), the attacker can and does use manipulation tactics to further intimidate, humiliate, blackmail and/or groom his or her victim.[4]

It is important to understand that a physiological response to assault in no way indicates that the victim enjoyed the assault any more than a male or female victim not responding to an assault (freezing) means there was consensual sex.

---

2. *https://slate.com/human-interest/2014/04/male-rape-in-america-a-new-study-reveals-that-men-are-sexually-assaulted-almost-as-often-as-women.html*

3. *The One in Six Statistics. http://1in6.org/get-information/the-1-in-6-statistic/*

4. *https://sapac.umich.edu/article/53*

As painful as the 'not believing' women issue has been for female victims of sexual assault, the 'hero' and 'machismo' attitude about men has made it nearly impossible for men to speak out. If a heterosexual boy or man is sexually assaulted by a female, he is mocked. If assaulted by another male, he will be called gay. If a homosexual boy or man is assaulted by another male, he probably *wanted it*. Worse, some will say that if he is gay, *how is it even rape*?

In 2017, when the famously buff actor and former NFL player Terry Crews revealed in an interview that he had been sexually assaulted by a Hollywood executive, the world was stunned. He defied the stereotype of the male sexual assault victim on multiple levels.

He was Terry Crews! *Who would dare try to assault Terry Crews?*

Answer: Sexual assault is about power, not strength. In this case, the Hollywood executive had the power and he knew it. According to Crews, as the executive assaulted him, Crews was powerless. In essence, he froze, fearing being ostracized. The assault was deliberate and designed to shock.

But he's Terry Crews! *If it really happened, why not just knock the guy out?*

Answer: Proving once again that sexual assault is about power, the assault took place in front of the executive agent's wife. Clearly, the agent wanted both Crews and his own wife to understand the power that he held as a Hollywood big-shot. As if to say, *'See, Darling! I can own this man.'* Both the woman and Crews were stunned into silence – a predator's dream. When Crews recovered, he had the fleeting thought a pummeling his abuser but then feared he would be arrested, imaging a headline that might read: "240-pound black man stomps out Hollywood honcho." And therein lies yet another power play predators rely upon: I am powerful. Do you really want to challenge me?[5]

But he's Terry Crews! *He's not just strong; he's powerful, too! He owns Hollywood. Everyone loves him. Why not speak out?*

Answer: Victims are victims. Male, female, big, small, strong, wealthy, poor, CEOs and Hollywood stars or just the guy next door, all carry the emotional scars from an assault that range from fear, anxiety, depression to guilt, confusion, and/or shame. These devastating

---

5. https://www.theguardian.com/film/2017/oct/11/actor-terry-crews-sexually-assaulted-by-hollywood-executive

emotions are carried by most victims throughout their lives, often being triggered by different sights, smells, sounds, words, even physical attributes of different people that might mirror that of their attacker. In the case of Terry Crews, however, we are fortunate that he was triggered by the Harvey Weinstein scandals and the #MeToo movement. On October 10, 2017, Crews tweeted, "This whole thing with Harvey Weinstein is giving me PTSD. Why? Because this kind of thing happened to ME." This revelation was as astonishing as it was empowering for other victims. It can happen to anyone – even Terry Crews.

But he's Terry Crews! Who would ever make fun of him being assaulted?

Answer: For those who have been in denial about just how demeaning and ignorant people can truly be, the astonishing revelation of Terry Crews exposed that, too. Comedian D.L. Hughley, who supposedly felt so compassionate toward a young lady he saw sexually assaulted that he wrote an op-ed piece about it in 2012, thought it appropriate to make fun of Terry Crews. Rapper 50 Cent and music mogul Russell Simmons, who both have a history of mistreating women through their music, lyrics, and behaviors with multiple charges of sexual assault and sexual harassment charges between them, both laughed at Crews' experience.

While ignorance abounded, Crews let them have it. He publicly challenged them all. In one particular tweet, Crews posted: You @50cent @unclerush and @tariqnasheed have decided my sexual assault was hilarious, whereas there are a whole generation of black women and men who don't think it's funny. ABUSERS PROTECT ABUSERS but they MOCK SURVIVORS as well. When you see me, keep it moving.[6] While the others backed down (no doubt pressured by tremendous public support for Crews) producer Tariq Nasheed continued his assault on Crews with, "I don't know why actor Terry Crews is so mad at me. He sure didn't have that same energy when he let that white man grab his crotch."

This pathetic response, which only turned fans against Nasheed, is the perfect example of why so many victims do not speak out.

He's Terry Crews. Sure, he could have beaten the agent to a pulp. But that's not what sexual assault is about. To repeat, sexual assault is more than just that horrible moment in time. It is an act, an assault, an aggression that leaves a mark on a single person and all of humanity. Although the

---

6. *https://www.usatoday.com/story/life/people/2019/01/28/terry-crews-celebs-mocked-his-sexual-assault-metoo-movement-dl-hughley-50-cent/2699273002/*

agent was fired and Crews took legal action against him, it was not until other victims came forward during the height of the #MeToo movement that Crews – this huge, former athlete, muscle-bound guy – mustered the courage to speak publicly. "I didn't go public right away. I gave them time to rectify the situation. I wanted them to get rid of this man," said Crews of the agent and the agency where he had been employed. "This was pre-#MeToo, if I would have gone to the police, I would have been laughed out of the precinct. This was also a time when people believed that you as a man couldn't be sexually assaulted. It was impossible to get anyone to believe."[7]

#BelieveSurvivors only works when it includes everyone.

---

7. *https://www.indiewire.com/2019/07/terry-crews-thanks-women-me-too-1202156051/*

17

ARE YOU PERCEIVED AS A VICTIM?

Before we move on to self-defense, it is important to speak about two other groups who are victimized more than the general population yet often remain silent: Black girls and women, and members of the LGBTQ communities.

Not only do black females experience higher rates of sexual violence, but they are less likely to report because of widespread institutional and historical racism. "If I could say one thing to other Black survivors right now, it would be, 'You matter and there is help,'" said a survivor and RAINN Speakers Bureau member. Members of LGBTQ communities in the U.S. face higher rates of sexual violence than the general population but report less because of fear of being judged or not believed or even harassed.[1]

It is worth repeating here: #BelieveSurvivors only works when it includes **everyone**.

So how can we stop being victims?

The more exposure you get to physical self-defense, the more you move, the more you practice, the more *real* this book and its scenarios will become for you. While victims will often say, "It happened so quickly," a more seasoned fighter will be able slow down the assault in her mind to react appropriately.

SCENARIO 15: THE BLINDSIDE ATTACK

Imagine walking out to your car late at night. You hear a sound, turn, and see a man running straight toward you. In an instant, you are confused. *Is he coming at me? What is happening? Did I do something?*

---

1. *https://www.rainn.org/*

In real life, a young violin instructor in Houston, Texas, headed back to her car following the last lesson of the evening. As it happened, there had been no place to park when she initially arrived at work and, so, pressed for time, she parked around the corner. In the daylight, the spot had not seemed too bad but now, in an unlit area and alone, she realized how bad the neighborhood really was.

Typically, she was gone by this time but two additional make-up lessons with students and the time change had suddenly left her in the dark. What she had not known until that very moment was that this area was known to police for drug problems.

WHAT SHOULD SHE HAVE DONE?

She should have had the last family give her a ride to her car.

She should have insisted that the owner of the studio secure safe, well-lit parking spaces for his employees.

WHAT SHE DID DO

What she did, however, was amazing.

When she turned to see the man running toward her, she dropped her bag filled with music sheets, her purse, and various items that only encumbered her. She dropped back into a fighting stance and as the man descended upon her, she drew back her beloved (hard case) violin and walloped the guy.

He yelped and staggered sideways upon impact.

Because she had taken over a dozen self-defense seminars, had learned to break boards with her hands and literally grew up in kickbox classes, she knew exactly what to do. In fact, she reported that "everything slowed down," as she processed what was happening:

1. *I'm being attacked.*
2. Guards up. Self-defense.
3. *Here he comes.*
4. She used her violin case like a baseball bat, swung hard and won.
5. She did not scream; she roared.

A Note from the Author: In full disclosure, the young woman in this scenario is this author's daughter. She took martial arts classes as both a child and young adult, for more than 20 years she's taken my kickbox classes, and even acted as my 'attacker' in self-defense lectures. She knew what to do and did it. Yet, as soon as she assured me that she was okay, that she had contacted the police, that she had given a description, and that she was safely on her way home … I laid into her on what she had done wrong. Even with all her experience and strength, she was lucky. True self-defense is about heading off potential problems. She knew better than to park in an unfamiliar territory; she knew better than to walk alone in the dark, but I also felt lucky that she knew what to do in an attack. As the brilliant Sun Tzu once said, "In the midst of chaos, there is also opportunity." Just as in the case of Leigh Ann discovering her roar, my daughter's constant practice had allowed her to process what was happening to her, break it down, and react (using her violin) in a manner that may have just saved her life.

WHAT WOULD YOU HAVE DONE?

Truly consider this scenario. Out of the darkness, a man is suddenly running right at you. In this case, the police believe the man was actually running for her oversized bag. There had been several reports of purse-snatching and robberies in that particular area. But how would you have reacted to this sudden ambush?

Run? Scream? Freeze?

Composure is a form of self-defense.

Just as you were asked to practice your yell in Chapter Eleven, practice your tone. You tone could change everything in an instant.

PERCEPTION – ARE YOU A VICTIM?...WHEN THE ATTACKER IS A STRANGER

In self-defense, perception really is everything. Your potential attacker has chosen you for a reason. Think about this: Of all the females in your school, on your team or in the neighborhood; of all the women at your work or on the college campus; of all the joggers or walkers outside on the trails, he chose *you*.

Those who sexually assault and/or harass are cowards; they are opportunists who choose a victim who cannot or will not fight back, cannot or will not yell, cannot or will not report them.

Take a moment and look at yourself as a bad guy might.

How do you look as you walk around while shopping, at work, in school or exercising? Is your head down? Are you distracted?

Are you quiet?

Do you appear shy? Insecure?

Do you give eye contact?

When Leigh Ann turned and charged the man whom she feared was stalking her, barking like a dog, she was terrified. She had no idea if he had a weapon, if he meant her serious harm or not, but she had felt threatened and was determined to defend herself.

Your voice, your posture, and your eye contact are you first line of defense.

Awareness is Armor is titled as such for a reason. You have to protect you. You have to be your first line of defense. How you sound, how you act and react to someone coming too close to you tells your would-be bad guy all that he (or she) needs to know about you.

PERCEPTION – ARE YOU A VICTIM?...WHEN THE ATTACKER IS A FRIEND

SCENARIO 12: A DIFFERENT KIND OF BLINDSIDE ASSAULT

Imagine you are spending the night at a friend's house or away at college, or perhaps you and your coworkers are attending a convention in a hotel when you are assaulted by someone you know and like. At least, you thought you knew and liked this person.

Suddenly, this friend pushes his way into your room and you are assaulted.

In this real-life scenario, a young college student is awakened by a friend who has locked himself out of his own dorm room. He is drunk but they are also friends so when he knocked on her door, asking to stay with her, she did not hesitate. As soon as he got into the room, however, things changed dramatically. Using his size and strength against her, the woman is pushed back against her own bed and raped by someone she had considered a very good friend.

She is confused, horrified, then enraged.

THE ALL-TOO COMMON RESPONSE

This scenario is far more common than most people expect. Across the globe, there are countless stories of women who were assaulted by a boss or co-worker in a hotel, a girl or woman assaulted by a friend's boyfriend or husband previously thought of as 'safe' because he was otherwise attached, a girl or woman who is raped by a trusted family friend.

Because of this, the victim is confused.

Remember that predators are opportunists and strategists. Bosses and employees rely on the victim worrying about her own reputation, losing her job, being demoted or ostracized at work. Husbands, boyfriends, stand-out athletes and popular members of the community rely on their own standing, certain they can spin their own version of what happened. *She threw herself at me! Yeah, I mean, I broke down and messed around with her. I know I shouldn't have but now she's crying 'rape' and that never happened!*

And far more often than not, alcohol is involved.

Victims then blame themselves for being drunk.

Victims make excuses for their attacker's behavior *because* he was drunk.

WHAT SHE DID

In this particular scenario, the victim had been asleep. She had not been out partying or misbehaving. Still, her reaction is all too common.

Initially, though she was angry, she recognized that he was drunk. She offered up his excuses before he could even dream them up himself. She worried that he could be expelled. She didn't want to "ruin his life"; she just felt she needed some kind of justice. But what?

Days passed and when she got nothing, she talked to a few friends.

Quickly, the word spread on campus that "I was the kind of girl who had sex, then cried 'rape' when I didn't like it." Further devastation came when her supposed friends chose to believe her rapist. And because she was so ashamed of being the girl who had sex, then called it rape, she let it drop. She never reported it to campus authorities or to the police.

Before suggesting what she should have done, let's turn this on you:

WHAT WOULD YOU DO?

In this real scenario, someone asked why she hadn't yelled for help. The answer is, she froze. It is infuriating and humiliating to her that she froze but that was what happened.

If this had been you, would you have yelled? *What* would you have yelled?

Although this *friend* was drunk, would you have been able to hit him over the head with something to ward him off if need be? If you could, you would then be able to run into the dorm's hallways calling for help once he stumbled backwards.

Or would you be too fearful? Would you freeze?

Would you use his drunkenness as a pass for assaulting you? Or would you have reported the rape to the police? Would you tell your friends and classmates that he had raped you? If not, why not?

Who would come to mind first? Would you think of the friends who would judge you or your parents who might want to pull you from school? Would you worry about your rapist *friend* and how this might destroy his life? Maybe you fear a boyfriend or husband learning that you had been raped would suddenly feel differently about you?

No one can tell you (the victim) how to feel but, remember that you are your last defense. While the physical assault is over, the emotional and psychological assault is still on.

WHAT SHE SHOULD HAVE DONE

Let's look at what would have been most ideal in this scenario. The rape has occurred. We will not review it any other way because, in this case, it does not help the victim. She trusted a friend, was assaulted, then froze. We cannot change those facts. This is still a self-defense book so … let's defend.

After the assault, as soon as she was able to move, it would have been best for her to run into the hall, calling for help. An immediate call for help would have alerted many witnesses to both her state of being – agitated, scared, hurt — and his – drunk and in a room in which he did not belong. The argument that she is just *the kind of girl* who cries rape changes dramatically had she run into the hall, calling for help, escaping her rapist. But again, if your attacker had once been a friend, how would you have reacted?

SCENARIO 16: BE SAFE ... HIRE A DRIVER!

Imagine that you are out with friends when you decide to call an Uber. Perhaps you have an early class or appointment the next morning, but your friends still want to stay out or maybe you've had a little too much to drink and decide to be safe and call for a ride. Whatever the situation, you simply locate a car using your Uber or Lyft app and wait.

In this real-life scenario, that is what Samantha Josephson did. The 21-year-old college student hopped into a car she believed she had summoned. It was the last time anyone saw her. In reality, she had mistakenly opened to car door of the wrong car and simply stepped in. The driver, a man who would ultimately rape and kill her, had been cruising around looking for a victim. If not already horrible enough, it was later learned that his car had been rigged so that the doors could not be opened from the inside. When Josephson realized her error, it was too late. She was trapped.

WHAT SHOULD SHE HAVE DONE?

We cannot bring Samantha Josephson back. Like all the women profiled in this book, there is no judgement. Terrible, costly mistakes were made but none reflect the character of the victim. In this case, however, we can use what happened to Josephson as a lesson.

We can presume she was on autopilot. She had summoned a car, saw one that matched the description she was looking for and then operated on pure trust that the driver was a good, solid citizen. Known to her friends and family as Sami, sweet and warm, Sami could not have imagined that she stepped into the car of the worst kind of predator.

She should have opened the back door and paused: *Is this my driver? Is this the right car?*

She should have taken a moment to look at his driver identification which must be in full view: *Are you [name of driver]?*

And then, she should have let the driver see her communicating with someone via call or text that she was stepping into the car of (example), Joe Smith, a black Impala.

WHAT SHOULD HAVE NEVER HAPPENED

Sami should never have parted ways alone from her friends at 2 a.m. outside a bar. For that matter, Sami should have never parted ways from her friends – period. Yet everyday friends let a friend go off with a boy, a strange man, get into an unknown car or walk home alone.

We know better. We know that there is a risk each time we do this but we 'hope and pray' and throw caution (and our lives) to the wind.

At a vigil in Sami's honor, Mr. Josephson spoke to his daughter's friends and fellow students, saying, "You guys need to travel together." Truer words could not have been spoken.[2]

WHAT WOULD YOU HAVE DONE?

It is so important to be honest here. If you had gone out with friends but now were suddenly tired or irritated or sick or just really wanted to go home but you friends wanted to stay, what would you do?

What if you met the greatest guy in the world and he begged you to take a walk with him before he had to leave?

How often have you ever gotten into an Uber or Lyft without hesitation?

How many times have you ever been in an Uber, Lyft or taxi and simply texted the entire time?

Even once – just once – could cost you everything.

SCENARIO 17 – HOME, SAFE, AND NOT-SO-SOUND

In this real-life scenario, a woman in New Jersey knew she had had too much to drink and called an Uber to pick her up but upon delivering her *safely* outside her home, he then raped her in the backseat of his car.[3] In Miami, after police apprehended the driver who raped a woman who had also been intoxicated, he admitted that he purposefully targeted women who were or appeared to be drunk. It was, he had bragged to police, "one of the perks to being an Uber driver."[4]

---

2. https://www.washingtonpost.com/crime-law/2019/03/31/she-thought-she-had-gotten-into-her-uber-police-say-hours-later-hunters-found-her-body/

3. https://www.nj.com/mercer/2019/12/uber-driver-sexually-assaulted-woman-in-car-after-driving-her-home-from-bar-cops-say.html

4. https://www.miaminewtimes.com/news/uber-driver-who-raped-woman-he-picked-up-in-wynwood-says-its-one-of-the-perks-of-driving-for-uber-10814630

While Uber is being used in this example, please note that statistically speaking, the number of assaults is equal between Lyft and Uber drivers. Predators are everywhere.

Alcohol is one of the most common components of these kinds of assaults, but there are hundreds upon hundreds of stories of completely sober passengers becoming victims of rape, unwanted touching, and/or harassment.

WHAT WOULD YOU DO?

Imagine that you attended a party with friends. It was a Sweet 16 party where you danced, played games then, upon your word to your parents, took an Uber home. Because it is assumed that Uber drivers are safe, the parents agreed. There was no alcohol, no drugs. It was just a fun party celebrating another friend's birthday.

On the way home, however, the driver takes the car in the opposite direction. Despite your protests, despite saying you just want to go home, the driver goads you into coming back to his house "for a drink." No matter what you say, he won't stop and he won't listen.

In this real-life scenario, a 15-year-old girl suddenly understood that she was in very big danger.

WHAT SHE DID

Sober and clear-minded, she insisted that she had to go to the bathroom and begged for them to stop at a McDonalds. Luckily for her, he stopped whereupon she was able to call for help.

WHAT SHE COULD AND SHOULD HAVE DONE

While her plan worked (and good for her!), she could have been even more proactive. With the very tool she used to call for an Uber, she could have simply dialed 911, then continued to ask the driver to please "stop," "let me out," and state again, "I just want to go home." A 911 operator, upon hearing this, is trained to alert officials and track her call.

Had the driver refused to stop at McDonald's, police would have already been on their way to rescue the girl who would have still been on her secret 911 call.

Not only adults but children, preteens, and teenagers need to understand that it is imperative to:

1. First open the door, lean in and confirm the driver is the person hired. This means asking for both a verbal confirmation of "What is your name?" and making sure the picture on the driver's license matches that of the person driving (and that the person driving matches the picture your Uber app sent you of your driver, along with his vehicle's make, model, and license plate).

2. Let the driver see/hear you confirming this information with someone on your phone.

3. If possible, remain on an open line talking to a friend or relative who can then track the progress of the trip with you. This lets the driver know that everything is being recorded and documented.

It is important to analyze each scenario to make you think of how you can respond but, even more importantly, how you think you might have responded before reading this book. The first true step to self-defense is self-critique.

It is also important to look at different scenarios and discuss the crime as it happened. Most definitely, self-defense is about heading off an assault, but it doesn't always work that way. Though difficult to read stories in which the victim was raped and/or killed, we need to pay attention to what happened (as we know the details).

We can never bring Sami or Missy back, but we can continue to keep their memories alive by learning from them. And for survivors, no matter how horrific the crime, it is important to remember that you are a survivor. Defending yourself is not a one-time event but, much like learning the art of self-defense, is an on-going journey that you should practice for the rest of your life. You must know how to defend yourself following an assault as well. As a survivor, you will be called upon to find your voice and continue your fight, whether in the legal system and/or for your own well-being.

Before 2014, singer Lady Gaga revealed to the world that she had been a victim of assault. In fact, she had been repeatedly raped by a record producer. What was not surprising to learn was Gaga's reaction. She blamed herself. She kept it a secret. She suffered immeasurably. Her story is a perfect example of how prevalent and powerful victim-blaming is, to the extent that she victim-blamed herself.

"Because of the way that I dress, and the way that I'm provocative as a person, I thought that I had brought this on myself in some way; that it was my fault," she said. She was just 19 years old, a rising star, raped by a man who was supposedly mentoring her. For seven years, she kept this terrible pain and shame to herself. "I didn't know how to accept it. I didn't know how not to blame myself, or think it was my fault. It was something that really changed my life. It changed who I was completely."[5] In 2016, she revealed that as a result of the trauma, she had developed PTSD and began to experience a host of physical and medical issues.

Only when the singer sought professional help and later, began talking about it, did the healing begin.

The truth is sexual assault can and does happen to anyone, no matter their appearance, age, sex, religion, socio-economic status, how they dress or where they live. But this act of violence from a coward does not define who and what you are.

In 2019, when Lady Gaga won an Oscar for 'Shallow,' from *A Star Is Born*, the honor also brought reminders of her past. A reporter asked, 'When you look at that Oscar, what do you see?" The singer responded that she saw, "A lot of pain." She had gone through so much to get to that point but like Chanel Miller, she persevered. In 2020, Lady Gaga would tell Oprah, "I kept going, and that kid out there or even that adult out there who's been through so much, I want them to know that they can keep going, and they can survive, and they can win their Oscar. I would also beckon to anyone to try, when they feel ready, to ask for help. And I would beckon to others that if they see someone suffering, to approach them and say, 'Hey, I see you. I see that you're suffering, and I'm here. Tell me your story.'"[6]

You are not alone.

#MeToo

#BelieveSurvivors

---

5. *https://www.thespec.com/whatson-story/5178068—swine-lady-gaga-tells-howard-stern-she-was-raped/*

6. *https://www.harpersbazaar.com/celebrity/latest/a29713019/lady-gaga-ptsd-sexual-assault/*

18

IT'S GO TIME!

At last! The instructional guide to self-defense. If you can remember even half of what you have read in this book, you are already leaps and bounds ahead of most people. But do not let that give you false confidence. Reading, listening to, and learning about self- and situational awareness is a fantastic start. It is your entry into true self-defense.

The next step is up to you. Begin your own research to find a martial arts studio or local police department that offers self-defense for women. Do not be shy about interviewing the owner and/or instructors about their teaching methods, current and past students. Ask for a few references and call them. Talk to other women who have been through the course(s) and specifically ask, "What *didn't* you like about the class?" and "What *didn't* you like about the instructor's teaching style?"

While this book could certainly outline different self-defense moves, reading does not equal doing. You need to practice the moves over and over; you need to go against opponents of different sizes; you need to understand spatial awareness. This can only come from hand-to-hand and/or hand-to-foot contact.

Our last scenario comes from a student in one of my workshops.

SCENARIO 18 – I'LL WALK YOU TO YOUR DOOR

Imagine that you've gone on a date with a pretty cute guy. You'd met only briefly before he asked you out for dinner, but you agreed based upon first appearances. On the actual date, however, you catch a bad vibe, a funny feeling about the man and make an excuse about not feeling well.

There is nothing specific that he has said or done to make you feel uncomfortable, but you just know you want to go home. When you say as much, he is clearly disappointed but insists on driving you back, noting, "I am a gentleman."

The ride home is cordial and your date even chats about music and movies. As soon as you get home, however, he seems a little too pushy. You just want out of the car, but he insists that he should walk you to your door. Again, he reminds you that it is something any true gentleman would do.

In this real-life scenario, Rashida was reluctant. She said she just wanted to open the car door and run but told herself, "I'm almost home. I told myself, 'Just let him walk you to your door and then it will be over.'"

As they entered her apartment building, he asked for her keys. She hesitated. "I didn't want to hand over my keys but he kept saying he wanted to escort me to my door, open it for me, stuff like that." At that point, Rashida admits, she was worn down by his gentlemanly manners and gave him her apartment key, thinking only that they were mere steps away from her closing her door on him forever.

WHAT REALLY HAPPENED

As soon as he opened the door, he smiled and extended an arm as though he was saying, 'Go inside' and 'Have a good night.' The moment she moved half a step inside her apartment, he shoved her inside and slammed the door behind her. He slammed her head against the wall inside the entryway, calling her terrible names, and began choking her.

She remembered thinking, "I didn't even have my keys!" Later, when she shared this story with the self-defense class, the bruises on her neck were still visible from where he had been choking her.

Spots were beginning to cloud her vision when she heard a voice: DON'T WASTE TIME TRYING TO PRY FINGERS FROM YOUR THROAT!

She remembered: When an assailant (typically male) is choking you, valuable time is lost when you (the victim) try to pull and pry strong fingers from your throat. As you lose oxygen, you also lose the fight. Instead, counter with an eye gouge or a throat punch or knee to the groin, if possible.

Predators are opportunists and do not want to fight. They do not want noise. They do not want to attract attention. And they do not want to have to engage in battle longer than necessary.

Rashida knew from exercises she had practiced in class that he was too close for a groin strike, but she also knew that her legs were very strong and if given a little more space, she could bring up a knee to put distance between them which would then allow her to scream "my fool head off!" To do this, she had to distract him.

She struck at his trachea with two jabbing fingers, as she had repeatedly practiced, to disable her attacker. Using a forearm strike, she could have done great damage to his windpipe (as it takes as little as five pounds of pressure to collapse the windpipe), but because of the close distance between them – and remember, at this point he is still choking her against a wall – the finger jab technique was all she had to work with.

And work, she did!

"He made, like, an 'akk' sound and kind of choked. I pushed him back, got my leg up between us and started yelling." At first, she said, she had little voice because he had been choking her, so she also reached up over her head, grabbed a picture frame and bashed it over his head. With even more distance between them, she executed another kick and was out into the hallway of her apartment building in seconds.

As tenants appeared, her attacker ran off but would later be apprehended by police.

WHAT SHE SHOULD HAVE DONE

After receiving a round of applause from her classmates, however, it was time to get serious. It never should have escalated to a woman being choked in her own apartment.

In the restaurant, she knew she wanted to get away from her date. Though many women would have had a difficult time doing this, she could have insisted on finding her own ride home, perhaps telling her date, "I don't want to ruin your night but I'm suddenly very anxious and uncomfortable. Please excuse me," and then leaving.

In the car on the way home, the moment the date pulled up to her apartment, she should have immediately exited the door, refusing to wait for his "I'm a gentleman" plea to walk her to her door. In this scenario, she was free and safe.

The real red flag is thrown

RED FLAG – there

In our classes, students learn strike zones and escape/evade tactics. The following is a very brief outline but will allow you something to go by while finding your own self-defense class:

FIRST LINE DEFENSE

1. **Definition of Self-Defense**: Taking whatever means necessary to stop an attack and put distance between yourself and your attacker!

2. **Objectives**:
   - Stop initial attack
   - Strike with maximum amount of force with maximum amount of damage
   - Draw attention to your situation

3. **Strike Zone**: Main strike areas are eyes, throat, groin, and knees

4. **Available weapons**: KNOW YOUR WEAPONS
   - Head
   - Elbows
   - Knees
   - Hands
   - Teeth

5. **Mental Awareness**: Be aware of your surroundings. Always be on the mental defense. (Translation: Put away the iPhone while walking in public.)

6. **Strengths and Weaknesses**: Know your limitations. Know your strengths and advantages. Your number one advantage is surprise and there is no second chance at surprise.

7. **Develop skills needed to defend**. This is where attending active classes where a kickbox instructor or a martial arts class build specific techniques and skillsets over time.

8. **Develop muscle groups used in this defense**. As you train beyond attending one or two seminars, your body will learn how to act and react in one-on-one combat (for isn't that what an attack is?) and you will be able to better execute (self-defense) moves if/when you are stronger. Consider fitness training an important aspect of her your self-defense training.

9. **Replace shock with action. Act; don't react**. As we discussed earlier, attackers rely on their victim to shrink back in surprise, to retreat and/or to beg for mercy rather than react. Learning *how* to react could save your life.

10. **Develop the attitude to win!**

- Do not fight to prevent robbery.

- Fight to save yourself or a loved one.

- Key Words to remember in self-defense:

- Ruthlessness

- Determination

- Physical Fitness

- Speed

- Surprise

- Warrior Mode – Never Quit!

- Do not hesitate to cause pain.

- Attacks can be brutal and savage:

- Your counterattack should be just as brutal and savage.

- Never let any concept of fairness cloud your willingness to strike any way you can!

- When you make a defensive move and cause your attacker to hesitate, lose focus or awareness, you MUST use those few seconds to attack or run!

- Never fight anyone on equal footing. Your attacker is not fighting fair. Nor should you. Use any means necessary to do serious damage and run.

- Anything, and everything, is a weapon.

- It is a surprise to your attacker if you fight. It is an even bigger surprise to your attacker if you know how to fight.

- If your attacker underestimates your ability to fight, he will be less cautious in his attack, and these initial moments of the attack are crucial!

- You can have your fingers in his eyes and your knee in his groin before he realizes he is in a fight, not simply an attack.

- A sharp/loud yell along with a well-placed kick or punch will produce results.

- YELLING IS A WEAPON!

- Screaming in fear is just panic. There is a difference.

- Animals growl on the attack – it's super scary and super effective!

- You are not a trained police officer. Do not think, "Control. Hold. Restrain." Think. "Immediate damage. Inflict injury. GET OUT!"

- No encounter should last more than 30 seconds.

- You are fighting to survive. The longer the fight, the greater your chance of losing.

- You have to want it more than he does!

- Expect to be hurt.

- Your body is not as frail or delicate as you have been led to believe. Your body was built to endure punishment if it has to.

- This is not the time to beg or try to negotiate. You have been chosen for a reason. It is – like it or not – officially "game on!" and you are in for the fight of your life. Your only motivation is to find a way to bring attention to yourself and get away.

REMEMBER:

- If an attacker is aroused by hate, anger, rage, lust or any other emotional drive, he has increased power and increased resistance to pain. Do not try to fight "fair." This is not fair.

- A man is more likely to continue an assault with a broken finger or after being struck in the face than he is after a crushing blow to the groin or the knee, an elbow to the windpipe, or an eye gouge.

- Go for critical targets:

- **Eyes** – eye attacks with the fingers or thumbs cause pain and obstruct vision.

- **Throat** – Regardless of physical strength, everyone reacts to loss of air. Go for windpipe!

- **Groin** – You do not have to use your foot or knee. There is no law against punching.

- **Go for the knee!** The knee joint is easy to hurt and it is vital for pursuing prey. Prey is what your attacker considers you to be! But 65 pounds of pressure brought sharply against a straight leg will crack the knee. Attacks to the side of the knee also work against ligaments and tendons. He can't chase you if you break his knee.

- **Secondary Targets:**
  - Bridge of the nose
  - Side of the neck
  - Shin or instep
  - Spine or kidney
  - Ears
  - Temple

As we bring this information to an end, this is only your beginning. What you do next is entirely up to you. We've discussed the importance of having a strong voice, of believing in your value, and of being situationally aware. While this book has been (and is!) about personal safety, it is also about living in the moment. It is about being present in your own life.

"YOU MAY NOT CONTROL ALL THE EVENTS THAT HAPPEN TO YOU, BUT YOU CAN DECIDE NOT TO BE REDUCED BY THEM." – MAYA ANGELOU

Today, we – as a society – live vicariously through social media, through funny memes and reality shows but these things are not your life. Take care of you. Practice your roar. Be aware of what is going on around you. Have the courage to speak up for others. Be your own champion.

"FEARLESSNESS IS LIKE A MUSCLE. I KNOW FROM MY OWN LIFE THAT THE MORE I EXERCISE IT THE MORE NATURAL IT BECOMES TO NOT LET MY FEARS RUN ME." – ARIANNA HUFFINGTON

Do not allow other people to manipulate, bully, coerce, peer-pressure or threaten you into doing something that makes you uncomfortable or scared. Do not allow yourself to be silence.

"NO ONE CAN MAKE YOU FEEL INFERIOR WITHOUT YOUR CONSENT." – ELEANOR ROOSEVELT

You read this book for a reason. You are destined to pilot your own life. Even if you have been the victim of an assault or any crime, this does not mean you are a victim in your own life. Believe in yourself and your worth and fight for it. When you learn to speak up, to speak out, to be heard, to care for yourself and others, you become a role model.

"ABOVE ALL, BE THE HEROINE OF YOUR LIFE, NOT THE VICTIM." – NORA EPHRON

NOTE FROM THE AUTHOR

Thank you for reading this book. It is my profound hope that you will find a boxing or kickboxing class, a martial arts studio or some empowering group that allows you to find your true self. Don't stop now!

When I teach self-defense and kickboxing, I always have my students break a board with their hand so that they can see just how strong they really are. I think it brings me more joy than anyone else. As a survivor of an assault, I know the feeling of helplessness and shame. *Was it my fault? Could I have done something to have prevented that?* But I also know the immense satisfaction of discovering how strong I am.

As soon as I bring out the board, I see terror in the eyes of most of my girls and women. As I walk them through the 'how' of breaking a board without hurting their hand, I also see the look of disbelief on their face. They truly do not think they have the strength to break the board.

What happens next is thrilling. Each and every time (for over 25 years now) a woman breaks her board, following the cheers and applause of her fellow classmates, comes that look! *Oh, that look.*

As soon as she sees her own hand smash through the board, adrenaline pumping through her body, and she straightens up to process, '*I just broke that board!*' she is exhilarated. She is momentarily, hilariously, gloriously, amazingly savage. She's a beast. She is wild-eyed and victorious.

I JUST BROKE THAT BOARD!

While I do **not** want you attempting any board break without professional instruction, I **do** want you to experience that moment when you realize you are strong. You **can** take care of yourself and you **are** your own champion!

Good luck. Be safe. Take care of yourself! Be aware – always.

— Alex

INDEX

www.ingramcontent.com/pod-product-compliance
Lightning Source LLC
LaVergne TN
LVHW061225060426
835509LV00012B/1428